Anthony Trollope: A Very Short Introduction

T0399132

VERY SHORT INTRODUCTIONS are for anyone wanting a stimulating and accessible way into a new subject. They are written by experts, and have been translated into more than 45 different languages.

The series began in 1995, and now covers a wide variety of topics in every discipline. The VSI library currently contains over 750 volumes—a Very Short Introduction to everything from Psychology and Philosophy of Science to American History and Relativity—and continues to grow in every subject area.

Very Short Introductions available now:

Available soon:

For more information visit our website

www.oup.com/vsi/

Dinah Birch

ANTHONY TROLLOPE

A Very Short Introduction

OXFORD
UNIVERSITY PRESS

OXFORD
UNIVERSITY PRESS

Great Clarendon Street, Oxford, OX2 6DP,
United Kingdom

Oxford University Press is a department of the University of Oxford.
It furthers the University's objective of excellence in research, scholarship,
and education by publishing worldwide. Oxford is a registered trade mark of
Oxford University Press in the UK and in certain other countries

Published in the United States of America by Oxford University Press
198 Madison Avenue, New York, NY 10016, United States of America

British Library Cataloguing in Publication Data
Data available

Library of Congress Control Number: 2024934959

ISBN 978-0-19-284562-7

Printed and bound by
CPI Group (UK) Ltd, Croydon, CR0 4YY

Links to third party websites are provided by Oxford in good faith and
for information only. Oxford disclaims any responsibility for the materials
contained in any third party website referenced in this work.

The manufacturer's authorised representative in the EU for product safety is Oxford
University Press España S.A. of el Parque Empresarial San Fernando de Henares,
Avenida de Castilla, 2 – 28830 Madrid (www.oup.es/en).

Contents

Preface

In July 1951, Harold Macmillan was a new minister in Winston Churchill's Cabinet. A demanding role, you might suppose—but his responsibilities did nothing to curb his addiction to Anthony Trollope's novels: 'I have finished *all* the Barchester series, ending with Last Chronicles of Barchester [*sic*]. This means that I have read all the clerical and all the political works again in the last few months, even weeks. This must stop. Trollope *is* a drug.' A generation later, the Labour politician Alan Johnson was similarly appreciative: 'Trollope's literary genius is, in my view, unquestionable.' Trollope's readers are diverse, and they are exceptionally loyal.

There are good reasons for their enthusiasm. Trollope's characters are sharply drawn, his plots are compelling, his evocation of Victorian Britain is engagingly vivid, and he is often irresistibly funny. Above all, he is enjoyable. But he provides more than escapism. He invites readers to share his creative process, as his characters move through their dilemmas and difficulties and make, or fail to make, the decisions that will define their lives. Trollope has no faith in the absolutes of virtue and vice, and even his most unpleasant characters are generally presented with a measure of compassion (there are exceptions—Obadiah Slope, the repellent chaplain who slides through the pages of the Barchester novels, is one). He rarely condemns, but he is a tireless judge, and he draws his readers into the challenging issues that haunt his writing. How is power to be properly exercised? What is the right relation between men and women? Why do so many people seem intent on destroying their own happiness? How is the need for progressive reform to be balanced with the claims of tradition? These are questions that continue to matter. Trollope offers no simple answers, but his fusion of entertainment with the power to make his readers think has not diminished.

Acknowledgements

I'm grateful to OUP's Luciana O'Flaherty and Imogene Haslam for their generous help and guidance, and to the peer reviewers who provided exceptionally thoughtful and constructive advice. I owe a great deal to many colleagues and friends who have discussed Anthony Trollope with me over the years and have contributed to the preparation of this book, including Dominic Edwardes, Kate Flint, Hilary Fraser, Hermione Lee, Francis O'Gorman, Rick Rylance, Nicolas Shrimpton, and Helen Small. My deepest gratitude goes to my husband, Sid Birch, for his untiring encouragement and support as this book took shape.

List of illustrations

Note on references and editions

Quotations from Anthony Trollope's novels and autobiography are taken from the World's Classics series and are reproduced with the permission of Oxford University Press. Chapter references appear parenthetically in the text. For other sources quoted in the text, together with suggestions for further reading, see the 'References and further reading' section at the end of the volume.

The American Senator, ed. John Halperin (Oxford: Oxford University Press, 2008)

An Autobiography and Other Writings, ed. Nicholas Shrimpton (Oxford: Oxford University Press, 2016)

Ayala's Angel, ed. Julian Thompson (Oxford: Oxford University Press, 1986)

Barchester Towers, ed. John Bowen (Oxford: Oxford University Press, 2014)

The Bertrams, ed. Geoffrey Harvey (Oxford: Oxford University Press, 1991)

Can You Forgive Her?, ed. Dinah Birch (Oxford: Oxford University Press, 2012)

Castle Richmond, ed. Mary Hamer (Oxford: Oxford University Press, 1989)

The Claverings, ed. David Skilton (Oxford: Oxford University Press, 1986)

Cousin Henry, ed. Julian Thompson (Oxford: Oxford University Press, 1987)

Doctor Thorne, ed. Simon Dentith (Oxford: Oxford University Press, 2014)

The Duke's Children, expanded edition, ed. Stephen Amarnick (Oxford: Oxford University Press, 2020)

The Eustace Diamonds, ed. Helen Small (Oxford: Oxford University Press, 2011)

An Eye for an Eye, ed. John Sutherland (Oxford: Oxford University Press, 1992)

The Fixed Period, ed. David Skilton (Oxford: Oxford University Press, 1993)

Framley Parsonage, ed. Francis O'Gorman and Katherine Mullin (Oxford: Oxford University Press, 2014)

He Knew He Was Right, ed. John Sutherland (Oxford: Oxford University Press, 2008)

John Caldigate, ed. N. John Hall (Oxford: Oxford University Press, 1993)

The Kellys and the O'Kellys, ed. W. J. McCormack (Oxford: Oxford University Press, 1982)

Kept in the Dark, ed. G. W. Pigman (Oxford: Oxford University Press, 1992)

Lady Anna, ed. Stephen Orgel (Oxford: Oxford University Press, 2008)

The Landleaguers, ed. Mary Hamer (Oxford: Oxford University Press, 1993)

The Last Chronicle of Barset, ed. Helen Small (Oxford: Oxford University Press, 2014)

The Macdermots of Ballycloran, ed. Robert Tracy (Oxford: Oxford University Press, 2008)

Anthony Trollope

Marion Fay, ed. Geoffrey Harvey (Oxford: Oxford University Press, 1992)

Miss Mackenzie, ed. A. O. J. Cockshut (Oxford: Oxford University Press, 1988)

Mr Scarborough's Family, ed. Geoffrey Harvey (Oxford: Oxford University Press, 1989)

Orley Farm, ed. Francis O'Gorman (Oxford: Oxford University Press, 2018)

Phineas Finn, ed. Simon Dentith (Oxford: Oxford University Press, 2011)

Phineas Redux, ed. John Bowen (Oxford: Oxford University Press, 2011)

The Prime Minister, ed. Nicholas Shrimpton (Oxford: Oxford University Press, 2011)

Ralph the Heir, ed. John Sutherland (Oxford: Oxford University Press, 1990)

The Small House at Allington, ed. Dinah Birch (Oxford: Oxford University Press, 2014)

The Three Clerks, ed. Graham Handley (Oxford: Oxford University Press, 1990)

The Vicar of Bullhampton, ed. David Skilton (Oxford: Oxford University Press, 1988)

The Warden, ed. Nicholas Shrimpton (Oxford: Oxford University Press, 2014)

The Way We Live Now, ed. Francis O'Gorman (Oxford: Oxford University Press, 2016)

Chapter 1
Family and work

Uncertain beginnings

In his life as in his writing, Trollope advocated the moral and practical value of work. It was, he believed, the only path to personal fulfilment. Writing to the Australian George Rusden, who had like Trollope given long service as a civil servant, he noted that 'I can conceive of no contentment of which toil is not to be the immediate parent.' Throughout his fiction, men who could not or would not do their work in the world were seen as harmlessly ineffectual at best, and at worst dangerous. Women had different kinds of work to do, and Trollope saw their role as primarily domestic, their work defined in relation to the family.

These apparently simple convictions fragment into a series of challenging questions in Trollope's novels. He grew uneasy about the constraints that hemmed in women's lives, and this became a recurrent theme. The opportunities open to men were wider. This freedom often brought its own difficulties, and Trollope's male characters often struggle with the burden of expectation, and the need to succeed in a ruthlessly competitive world. For those brought up to be gentlemen—always Trollope's highest category of human value—the choice of profession was not straightforward. How was the distinctive identity of a gentleman to be defended and an adequate income secured, in a period where the boundaries of rank and class were increasingly fluid?

These concerns are rooted in Trollope's troubled childhood and adolescence. Though he was born into an affluent family, his early years were shadowed by poverty and disappointment. His father, Thomas Anthony Trollope, was an unsuccessful barrister and an equally unsuccessful farmer (see Figure 1). Anthony was sent to Harrow (a leading private school) as a day boy at the age of 7. The proximity of the family's farm meant that no fees were charged, but it also meant that he was scorned as a 'village boy'. Two years later, he began to attend Sunbury, a private school in Sussex, where he was just as unhappy.

Further difficulties followed when he entered Winchester, his father's old school. There was no money to pay the fees, a humiliating fact which was soon known among his fellow pupils. As an economy measure, Trollope returned to Harrow, for what he described in his autobiography as 'the worst period of my life. I was now over fifteen, and had come to an age at which I could appreciate at its full the misery of expulsion from all social intercourse. I had not only no friends, but was despised by all my companions … What right had a wretched farmer's boy, reeking from a dunghill, to sit next to the sons of peers,—or much worse still, next to the sons of big tradesmen who had made their ten thousand a-year?' (Chapter 1).

The family's approaching ruin was postponed by the labours of Trollope's resolute mother Frances, who—having failed to make money through her commercial enterprises in a four-year stay in America—forged a flourishing career for herself as a novelist and travel writer. Frances's achievements were remarkable, and were to become on important influence on Trollope. She taught her son that sustained application to the work involved in a writer's profession could lead to social status and a worthwhile income.

1. In the frontispiece to the first edition of *Orley Farm* (1862),
John Everett Millais depicts 'Julian Hill', the house (near Harrow)
that Trollope's parents adapted and enlarged to accommodate their
growing family.

But Frances could not rescue Trollope from his painful situation at Harrow, nor could she entirely restore the family's fortunes. In 1834, Thomas Trollope's beleaguered family was forced to move to Belgium to avoid imprisonment for debt, and Anthony, then a callow 19-year-old, was finally free of the torments of his schooling (he later published authoritative books on the classics—banishing any lingering notion that he could not claim a gentleman's education). There was some thought of his attending Oxford, but he failed to win the scholarships that might have made that possible. Eventually family connections led to a post in the newly established Post Office, and he began to work as a junior clerk in London.

The Post Office

The Post Office was eventually to provide Trollope with a fruitful career extending for more than 30 years. He became one of the ablest administrators in the civil service, entrusted with high-level missions in Britain and overseas, establishing postal treaties and working out routes, and implementing plans for effective operational procedures. He took his work seriously and was highly regarded by his colleagues, and is remembered for his introduction of the pillar-box into Britain (see Figure 2). Even after he stepped down from the Post Office in 1867 to concentrate on his literary work, he negotiated a new postal agreement with the United States. But in his early years as a clerk success of any kind seemed as distant as ever.

Trollope's starting salary (£90 a year) was insufficient for a young man living alone in London, and he fell into debt. As he recalled in his autobiography, he was often late for work and was 'always in trouble' (Chapter 3). But he was learning about the world, and many of his doleful early experiences in the office found their way into the substance of his fiction. He observed at first hand, and was never to forget, that financial stability and a steady purpose are necessary conditions for a fruitful life. His narratives repeatedly

2. London's first pillar-box (1855). Red pillar-boxes did not appear until 1874, and this pioneering example would have been painted green.

return to themes aligned with the traumas of his youth—the difficulty of finding the right work, alongside the need for money, the wish for money, the power of money, and the corrosive effect of debt.

The financial circumstances of these formative years also account for his lifelong interest in questions of inherited wealth, which figures prominently in much of his fiction. Trollope was not unique in this concern. At a time when social standing and financial security often depended on the money and property that was to be passed (or not) through the generations, the plots of many 19th-century novels turn on the hopes for inheritance, and the influence that lay in the hands of those who could dispense or withhold a family's accumulated resources.

Trollope's father had expected to inherit a substantial country house and associated estate in Hertfordshire, owned by his uncle, Adolphus Meetkerke, who was childless. Here would lie the solution to his financial problems. But Adolphus's wife died, and he soon remarried a much younger woman. Despite his years, Adolphus became the father of six children, and any prospect of an inheritance for Trollope's father vanished. This was, Trollope recalls in his autobiography, a 'final crushing blow' (Chapter 1), a disaster that casts a long shadow over the concerns of his mature fiction.

The loneliness of his early years encouraged Trollope to live in a world of imagined stories. In his autobiography, he recalls that

> I was always going about with some castle in the air firmly built in my mind... For weeks, for months, if I remember rightly, from year to year, I would carry on the same tale, binding myself down to certain laws, to certain proportions, and proprieties, and unities... There can, I imagine, hardly be a more dangerous mental practice; but I have often doubted whether, had it not been my practice, I should ever have written a novel. I learned in this way to maintain an interest in a fictitious story, to dwell on a work created by my own imagination, and to live in a world altogether outside the world of my own material life. In after years I have done the same,—with this difference, that I have discarded the hero of my early dream, and have been able to lay my own identity aside. (Chapter 3)

For all the intensity of his later working life as a civil servant and a novelist, and his emphasis on the practical routines of the working writer, the roots of Trollope's extraordinarily prolific output as a writer lay in the solitary life of the imagination.

Ireland

From the perspective of his professional progress, a crucial turning point came in 1841, when Trollope secured a post as a postal surveyor's clerk in central Ireland. Ireland had been formally assimilated into the new United Kingdom of Great Britain and Ireland in 1800, so that the Post Office had responsibility for managing postal services across the whole of the country.

Though Trollope continued to report to his seniors in London, Ireland's separate history and culture meant that his new duties took place in a context that was unlike anything he had previously experienced. His promotion became the means of escaping his money worries, and at last leaving his difficult early years behind. He was 26 years old—no longer a very young man, but young enough to make a fresh start. He seized the opportunity with enthusiasm, and Ireland became his primary home for the next 18 years.

With a novelist's instinct to impose order on life's untidiness, Trollope was later inclined to overstate the significance of his move to Ireland. His autobiography makes the liberation from the problems of his early career seem near-miraculous: 'From the day on which I set my foot in Ireland—all these evils went away from me' (Chapter 4). This was an overstatement. He learned more at school, and as a clerk in London, than he was later willing to admit, and he was necessarily feeling his way on first taking up his post. But his new position in Ireland, where he knew nobody and nobody knew him, enabled him to reinvent himself, escaping from the years of disappointment, and beginning to establish more productive habits. It was in Ireland that he took his responsibilities to the Post Office more seriously, and it was there that he began to publish fiction.

It was also in Ireland that he found a wife. He met Rose Heseltine, the daughter of a Rotherham banker, while they were both holidaying in Kingstown (now Dún Laoghaire), a coastal town near Dublin (see Figure 3). She was five years younger than Trollope, and had been brought up in solid middle-class comfort, with no aspirations to grandeur. Given the central importance of the vicissitudes of courtship and marriage in Trollope's fiction, we know frustratingly little about his own experience. In *Orley Farm* (1862), his advice to young men in search of a wife is brisk and down-to-earth: 'Dance with a girl three times, and if you like the light of her eye and the tone of voice with which she, breathless,

7

3. Rose Heseltine, Anthony Trollope's wife. This undated photograph is one of the few images of Rose to have survived.

answers your little questions about horseflesh and music—about affairs masculine and feminine,—then take the leap in the dark' (Chapter 33).

Perhaps this was how Trollope made up his mind to propose to Rose, just a fortnight after they met. They married in 1844, after a

8

two-year engagement, when Trollope was 29 years old, and the first child, Henry Merivale Trollope, was born in 1846. A second son, Frederick James Anthony Trollope, followed in 1847. The commitment was lifelong, but neither Trollope nor his wife chose to tell the world anything about its nature. His autobiography is defiantly reticent. 'My marriage was like the marriage of other people, and of no special interest to any one except my wife and me' (Chapter 4). What we do know is that the emotional security and sense of responsibility that followed his marriage helped to build Trollope's growing feeling that he had a place in the world.

Among the lasting consequences of Trollope's new and more sociable identity in Ireland was that it enabled him to discover the pleasures of hunting, a pursuit that became a lifelong passion. Like his marriage, Trollope's taste for hunting is mysterious. Nothing in his family background or early interests suggested that he would find the hunting field rewarding—'one of the great joys of my life', as he was to describe it in his autobiography (Chapter 4). It was an expensive and often dangerous sport, and it was difficult to fit into a busy professional life. Yet the hunt really mattered to Trollope, for reasons that he could not himself explain. It was an indulgence, but he also, rather oddly, describes it as a duty and a labour—like other aspects of his mature life:

> I have ever since been constant to the sport, having learned to love it
> with an affection which I cannot myself fathom or understand.
> Surely no man has laboured at it as I have done, or hunted under
> such drawbacks as to distances, money, and natural disadvantages.
> I am very heavy, very blind, have been—in reference to hunting—a
> poor man, and am now an old man. I have often had to travel all
> night outside a mail-coach, in order that I might hunt the next day.
> Nor have I ever been in truth a good horseman. And I have passed
> the greater part of my hunting life under the discipline of the
> Civil Service. But it has been for more than thirty years a duty to
> me to ride to hounds; and I have performed that duty with a

persistent energy. Nothing has ever been allowed to stand in the way of hunting,—neither the writing of books, nor the work of the Post Office, nor other pleasures. (Chapter 4)

Hunting was a demandingly physical occupation, removed from the daily routines of Trollope's arduous working life. Perhaps this was among its attractions. It also allowed him to observe interactions between men and women from different classes and backgrounds, sometimes in dramatic circumstances—for accidents were frequent, and sometimes serious. Hunting episodes appear regularly in Trollope's fiction, providing the means to move his plots in unexpected directions, but also giving a different and more unpredictable context for the exploration of his characters and their relationships, creating a freedom that would have been impossible in scenes set in the drawing-room or the office.

Starting to write

Encouraged by the example of his mother, Trollope had cherished the hope that he might become a novelist since his earliest days in the Post Office. He describes his literary ambitions in his autobiography:

I had often told myself since I left school that the only career in life within my reach was that of an author, and the only mode of authorship open to me that of a writer of novels ... Poetry I did not believe to be within my grasp. The drama, too, which I would fain have chosen, I believed to be above me. For history, biography, or essay writing I had not sufficient erudition. But I thought it possible that I might write a novel. I had resolved very early that in that shape must the attempt be made. But the months and years ran on, and no attempt was made. (Chapter 3)

Here too, Ireland provided both motive and opportunity. He was engaged to be married, with the obligations of a married man in prospect, and Irish landscapes and society were providing new imaginative stimulus. He describes a crucial encounter with the ruins of a country house: 'It was one of the most melancholy spots I ever visited ... while I was still among the ruined walls and decayed beams I fabricated the plot of *The Macdermots of Ballycloran*' (Chapter 4). In 1847, when he was about to turn 32, Trollope's first novel was published as a three-volume work by Thomas Newby, a notoriously dilatory and ungenerous publisher. Trollope expected little from this venture: 'I was sure that the book would fail, and it did fail most absolutely' (Chapter 4). Melodramatic and gloomy, and embedded in the social problems of Ireland, the novel was hardly calculated to make a strong entry into the market. But it was a start, and the reviews were not entirely discouraging.

Trollope soon tried again, this time with a comic novel and a different publisher (Henry Colburn, contacted through his mother's influence). *The Kellys and the O'Kellys* appeared in 1848, and though the critical reception was largely positive, this second novel also made no money. But Trollope, who had by no means abandoned his determined and increasingly successful efforts to build his career with the Post Office, was not prepared to give up on his second vocation as a writer. He was beginning to establish the patterns that would shape his mature approach to fiction—the lucid prose, shrewd character sketches, the use of letters, alongside an exploration of interactions between social groups with differing values and principles, in the context of financial skulduggery and courtship plots.

His third attempt, *La Vendée*—another commercial failure—was a historical novel about the royalist uprising against the French Republic in 1794, from which Trollope learned that he could not write fiction on the basis of distanced research among books and papers. Some degree of first-hand observation was essential to his creative impulse. Succeeding years demanded a focus on his Post Office duties, and Trollope was almost 40 years old before he achieved his first popular success with the first of the

Barsetshire novels. Like *The Macdermots of Ballycloran*, *The Warden* (1855) had its beginnings in an encounter with an atmospheric building. It was suggested by a walk in Salisbury—'one midsummer evening round the purlieus of the cathedral . . . from whence came that series of novels of which Barchester, with its bishops, deans, and archdeacon, was the central site' (Chapter 5). Trollope had found his voice as a novelist.

Success at last

Though it was only with the publication of *Barsetshire Towers* in 1857 that Trollope began to earn money from his fiction, the appearance of *The Warden* represents a pivotal moment in his life as a writer. He was still committed to his career in the Post Office, but he began to see real prospects of establishing himself in the literary world. Novels were not the only possible means of achieving these ambitions, and his next book, *The New Zealander*, was a broadly-based and often bitingly disparaging survey of British institutions. The title refers to an 1840 essay by the historian Thomas Macaulay, predicting that one day 'some traveller from New Zealand shall, in the midst of a vast solitude, take his stand on a broken arch of London Bridge to sketch the ruins of St Paul's'. Trollope approached William Longman with his manuscript. A more serious and prestigious publisher than either Newby or Colburn, Longman had published *The Warden*. He thought, probably correctly, that the acerbic tone of *The New Zealander* would damage Trollope's reputation. The book remained unpublished until 1972.

The New Zealander is a reminder of Trollope's keen engagement with current social, political, and scholarly issues. Alongside a prodigious quantity of fiction (47 novels and 42 short stories), he produced a substantial body of non-fiction over his long writing career—five travel books, three late biographies (*Thackeray* in 1879, *The Life of Cicero* in 1880, and *Lord Palmerston* in 1882), together with *The Commentaries of*

Caesar (1870), and a posthumously published autobiography. His range as a writer is astonishing.

These books were accompanied by a steady stream of articles, reviews, and letters for a range of periodicals and newspapers. Trollope was often critical of the power of the press, but journalism was important to him, and the thriving periodicals of the period, where Trollope's fiction was often first published in parts, were crucial to his relations with his reading public. Among his many professional initiatives was his three-year editorship of a periodical, *Saint Pauls Magazine* (1867–70), a role which, together with his ambition to become a Member of Parliament, prompted his resignation from the Post Office, and full-time dedication to a productive literary life.

What characterizes these varied publications and activities was an unrelenting commitment to a life of labour. A dedication to work was, for Trollope, where the meaning of his life was to be found, and also its happiness. He was not unique in this conviction. Many of his contemporaries shared his belief that disciplined work, essential to national prosperity, also lay at the centre of a life's fulfilment. 'A man perfects himself by working,' Thomas Carlyle claimed in *Past and Present* (1843), and many agreed (there was much more uncertainty about what would perfect a woman). But few had the energy and the creative confidence to carry this conviction to the extreme lengths demonstrated in the remarkable life and work of Anthony Trollope.

Chapter 2
Story and style

Style and purpose

Trollope claimed to place the highest value on a narrative style
that draws no attention to itself. His 1879 book on the novelist
William Makepeace Thackeray, whose work he greatly admired,
prompted him to reflect on literary language at some length.
'I hold that gentleman to be the best dressed whose dress no one
observes. I am not sure but that the same may be said of an author's
written language' (Chapter 9). Throughout his writing life, he
denies that his style, or any writer's style, is worthy of much scrutiny.

Trollope distances himself from the linguistic exuberances of
Charles Dickens, or Thomas Carlyle, or the heavily emotional
register of the popular romances or sensation fiction of the mid-
Victorian period. His language is measured and low-key, often
adopting the perspective of an interested observer as he presents
the nuances of character or scene for the reader's judgement.
'A novel in style should be easy, lucid, and of course grammatical.
The same may be said of any book; but that which is intended to
recreate should be easily understood,—for which purpose lucid
narrative is an essential' (Chapter 9).

In fact, Trollope's gentlemanly style is by no means as
straightforward as these blunt and down-to-earth remarks would

imply. He creates a narrative voice that demands the reader's participation in his characters' dilemmas and uncertainties, some of them reflecting the underlying tensions that shaped his own responses to the changing cultural and political conditions he saw around him. In his autobiography, Trollope identifies himself as an 'advanced Conservative-Liberal' (Chapter 16), balancing his inclination to welcome reform and progress, as he had done in his work as a ruthlessly efficient reforming civil servant in the Post Office, with his lingering commitment to older patterns of social value. His novels contend with changing constructions of the self in an increasingly individualistic and competitive world, and they reach no simple conclusions as to the lessons that might be learned from his stories.

He is, however, clear that lessons should be learned. Trollope never swerved from his conviction that fiction had an ethical responsibility, alongside what it owed to the entertainment of his readers and his own need (never far from his mind) to translate literary production into a regular income. He considers this question in his reflections on Thackeray: 'I should be said to insist absurdly on the power of my own confraternity if I were to declare that the bulk of the young people in the upper and middle classes receive their moral teaching chiefly from the novels they read' (Chapter 9).

Despite his defensive disclaimer, this is what Trollope believed. He observes that 'Thackeray thought that more can be done by exposing the vices, than extolling the virtues of mankind. No doubt he had a more thorough belief in one than the other' (Chapter 3). Trollope's approach was different, for he had no fixed belief in any absolute division between virtue and vice in his characters. Noting that 'a novelist has two modes of teaching—by good example or by bad' (Chapter 9), he composes complex and layered narratives that call on the reader to decide where the boundaries between good and bad examples might fall. This is a narrative pattern that is already apparent in

The Warden (1855), where the reader is asked to respond to
a series of demanding moral questions.

The Warden

The beginnings of success established by *The Warden* (1855)
settled Trollope's direction as a novelist working within the
conventions of domestic realism, with predominantly English
settings. Broadly speaking, his readers encountered a
recognizably contemporary world in his fiction, peopled with
characters drawn from a range of social groups within British
society, and with plots that revolve around credible (if often
dramatic) turns of events.

The Warden deals with the dilemmas surrounding the
lucrative wardenship of Hiram's Hospital (an ancient almshouse)
within the context of ecclesiastical politics, embedding the
courtship plot that was to become characteristic of
Trollope's fiction. The forceful young surgeon and social
reformer John Bold (his name reflects his nature) identifies
the substantial income that kindly Septimus Harding derives
from his post as Warden of Hiram's Hospital as an abuse,
eliciting the support of the press to expose a practice that he
sees as corrupt.

The situation is complicated by Bold's romantic relations
with Harding's daughter Eleanor, who eventually becomes his
wife. Trollope makes it clear that the income of the Warden is
indeed not proportionate to the work required by the post,
though Harding discharges his limited duties faithfully.
Bold is not wrong. But the outcome of the conflict is
ambiguous. Archdeacon Grantly, who urges Harding to resist
Bold's attack, is self-interested and overbearing. The press,
represented by Tom Towers, the ambitious journalist on the
staff of *The Jupiter* (recognizably *The Times*) who whips up
indignation about Harding's supposed malefactions, is primarily

motivated by his wish to generate a public scandal to benefit his own career. 'It is probable that Tom Towers considered himself the most powerful man in Europe; and so he walked on from day to day, studiously striving to look a man, but knowing within his breast that he was a god' (Chapter 14).

Despite its realistic narrative frame, *The Warden* contains more openly satirical material than was usual in Trollope's later novels, and contemporary writers are included among his targets. 'Mr Popular Sentiment' (who clearly represents Charles Dickens) turns the controversy over Hiram's Hospital into the theme of a new novel: 'Mr Sentiment is certainly a very powerful man, and perhaps not the less so that his good poor people are so very good; his hard rich people so very hard; and the genuinely honest so very honest' (Chapter 15). Dr Pessimist Anticant (Thomas Carlyle) weighs in with a vituperative pamphlet:

Dr Pessimist Anticant was a Scotchman, who had passed a great portion of his early days in Germany; he had studied there with much effect, and had learnt to look with German subtilty into the root of things, and to examine for himself their intrinsic worth and worthlessness. No man ever resolved more bravely than he to accept as good nothing that was evil; to banish from him as evil nothing that was good. 'Tis a pity that he should not have recognised the fact, that in this world no good is unalloyed, and that there is but little evil that has not in it some seed of what is goodly. (Chapter 15)

Neither Mr Sentiment nor Dr Anticant is prepared to recognize the nuances of the problem represented by the Warden's position. The elderly bedesmen who inhabit the almshouse, greedy for financial gain, find that Harding's eventual resignation of his wardenship represents only loss. No one, with the exception of Septimus Harding and his loyal daughter, behaves well. The process of reform, however necessary, is coloured with an elegiac sense of regret.

Author and reader

Trollope includes his readers as partners in the processes of reflection that lead to the rueful conclusions of *The Warden*, establishing a reciprocal relationship that persists and develops throughout his career. One of its distinctive characteristics is the openly shared understanding that what we are encountering is a novel, no matter how real the events and characters might seem. This is one of the ways in which Trollope takes us into his confidence, in a friendly and companionable manner. *The Warden*'s 'Conclusion' is an early example of this approach: 'Our tale is now done, and it only remains to us to collect the scattered threads of our little story, and to tie them into a seemly knot. This will not be a work of labour, either to the author or to his readers; we have not to deal with many personages, or with stirring events, and were it not for the custom of the thing, we might leave it to the imagination of all concerned to conceive how affairs at Barchester arranged themselves' (Chapter 21).

The notion of the reader as a kind of co-creator of the story, engaged with its proper resolution alongside the novelist, is essential to Trollope's method. He repeatedly appeals to our imagination and judgement, in matters small and large. Reflecting on the marital relations between the sanctimonious Archdeacon Grantly and his ever-sensible wife, he cuts Grantly's authority down to size by noting that it disappears once he retires to bed:

> Do we not all know some reverend, all but sacred, personage before whom our tongue ceases to be loud and our step to be elastic? But were we once to see him stretch himself beneath the bed-clothes, yawn widely, and bury his face upon his pillow, we could chatter before him as glibly as before a doctor or a lawyer. From some such cause, doubtless, it arose that our archdeacon listened to the counsels of his wife, though he considered himself entitled to give counsel to every other being whom he met. (Chapter 2)

This interweaving of story and authorial appeal ('Do we not all know...') establishes a sense of participatory ownership within the narrative ('our archdeacon') that has much to do with Trollope's popularity. Readers are led to feel that they are part of the creative process, on an equal standing with Trollope himself. We are invited into the narrative.

The Warden, a short novel, was published as a single volume, but most of Trollope's subsequent fiction first appeared in serial form. Periodicals of many different descriptions, with distinctive though sometimes overlapping readerships and varying price levels, became increasingly important to the creative and business practices of writers in the early and middle decades of the 19th century. Trollope's role as the founding editor of *Saint Pauls Magazine* meant that he was actively involved in this development. Much of his work—including most of his substantial output in the form of short stories—was first published in periodicals, though some serially published novels appeared in separately published parts.

Writers would adjust the tone and subject matter of their work to align with the expectations of a periodical's readership. In writing short stories for *Good Words*, for instance, a periodical (established in 1860) with a flourishing readership among evangelical and nonconformist audiences in the 1860s and 1870s, Trollope was careful not to affront the religious sensibilities of this particular market. Mally, the wild barefoot girl who is the Cornish heroine of the short story 'Malachi's Cove' (published in *Good Words* in 1864), is somewhat incongruously seen to be a regular church-goer, having 'submitted herself to the teaching of the clergyman at Tintagel'. This level of attention to the tastes and interests of specific audiences figures among the ways in which Trollope was able to build a wide readership, with an appeal that extended across differing social and cultural groups. As the market for fiction extended its reach in the middle decades of the 19th century, this strategy was important to his growing popularity.

Sensationalism

The 1860s, the period when the devout readership of *Good Words* was at its peak, was also the decade which saw the rise of sensation fiction. The emergence of sensation novels presented a particular challenge to Trollope's preferred model of understated gentlemanly good sense. With their characteristic focus on madness, drug-taking, and hidden crimes within contemporary domestic settings, sensation novels were deliberately distant from the more sober patterns of realism that had provided Trollope with his growing reputation. The rackety thrills of sensation fiction, with their roots in the mysterious doings of earlier Gothic fiction, were alien to the discreet values of an English gentleman, and the prominence of women within the genre, exemplified in the work of Ellen Wood (commonly known as Mrs Henry Wood) and Mary Braddon, further emphasized the distance between this phenomenon and Trollope's masculine ideals as a professional writer.

Trollope was particularly hostile to the dependence of the sensation plot on the concept of the sinister secret, hidden from both the characters of the novel and its readers, which he saw as a betrayal of the trust which should define the relation between author and reader. This is among the features of sensationalism that he explicitly condemns, describing it in *Barchester Towers* (1857) as a 'system which goes so far to violate all proper confidence between the author and his readers by maintaining nearly to the end of the third volume a mystery as to the fate of their favourite personage . . . is there not a species of deceit in this to which the honesty of the present age should lend no countenance?' (Chapter 15). Mary Braddon's extraordinarily popular *Lady Audley's Secret* (1862) was an influential example of a lucrative page-turner constructed on the principle of a carefully hidden secret, startlingly revealed in the final pages of the novel.

Trollope has no time for these narrative ploys, nor for the historically Gothic trappings of castles, abbeys, or villainous monks and nuns. As he tells his readers in *The Bertrams* (1859), 'I abhor a mystery. I would fain, were it possible, have my tale run through from its little prologue to the customary marriage in its last chapter, with all the smoothness incidental to ordinary life. I have no ambition to surprise my reader. Castles with unknown passages are not compatible with my homely muse. I would as lief have to do with a giant in my book—a real giant, such as Goliath—as with a murdering monk with a scowling eye' (Chapter 13).

However homely his muse, Trollope did not fail to notice the popular appeal of sensation fiction from the later 1850s onwards. Elements of its strategies increasingly found their way into his fictional practice. Just as he resists any absolute division between virtue and vice, he came to be sceptical about any attempt to reduce the novel into neat categories. He makes his position clear in his autobiography: 'There are sensational novels, and anti-sensational; sensational readers, and anti-sensational. The novelists who are anti-sensational are generally called realistic. I am realistic. My friend Wilkie Collins is generally supposed to be sensational...All this I think is a mistake...A good artist should be both, and both in the highest degree' (Chapter 12).

Brushes with adultery, violence, suicide, and murder are recurrent in Trollope's novels, as are examples of financial corruption. He repeatedly returns to the theme of mental imbalance that threatens to collapse into insanity—as in Josiah Crawley's bitter intransigence in *The Last Chronicle of Barset* (1867), George Vavasor's self-destructive behaviour in *Can You Forgive Her?* (1864), or Louis Trevelyan's obsessive jealousy in *He Knew He Was Right* (1869). Though he continues to keep his distance from women who wrote sensation fiction (it is not an accident that Wilkie Collins is named as its chief representative, rather than the leading female practitioners of the genre), his sympathy is always with victims of injustice, and his increasing concern with the injustices and oppression endured by women mean that his plots share the sensation novel's characteristic concern with women's social position.

John Caldigate (1879) explores the theme of bigamy, a favourite preoccupation of the genre; *Lady Anna* (1874) includes an obsessive mother who attempts to achieve her ambitions with the aid of a loaded gun; the compelling heroines of both *Orley Farm* (1862) and *The Eustace Diamonds* (1872) are secretive criminals. Plots which turn on forged documents, disputed legitimacy, or complex legal disputes proliferate. These sensational features are interwoven with the realism of minutely observed scenes that reflect the changing relations between social classes, or the shifts in political culture, or the interaction between the life of London and that of the provinces. Trollope was not a sensation novelist. Nevertheless, he was fully prepared to draw on the range of imaginative resources represented by its dramatic power.

Illustrations

Trollope is also consistently interested in the interaction between textual narrative and visual images. This concern is reflected in the vivid detail with which he describes his characters, and the landscapes and buildings in which their stories are set. He wants us to see the action of his fiction as it unfolds, as an essential feature of the way in which we understand and judge his characters and their behaviour. These visual perspectives are extended by the illustrations that regularly accompanied his texts. Novels for adults are now rarely illustrated, but in the Victorian period this was an established practice. 'What is the use of a book . . . without pictures or conversations?', as Alice remarked in the opening sentences of *Alice in Wonderland* (Chapter 1). Victorian readers were inclined to agree, and novelists and their publishers obliged by supplying both.

Full-page pictures were routinely included in the serially published parts of a novel, as part of the purchase price. Close working relations would sometimes develop between writers and their illustrators—as, for instance, in the fruitful partnerships between Dickens and George Cruikshank, John Leech, and Hablot Knight Browne ('Phiz'). The quality of the pictures included in his publications was important to Trollope, and to his readers. He worked with several illustrators, including Marcus Stone and Mary Ellen Edwards, but his favourite collaborator was the celebrated and successful artist John Everett Millais, who illustrated many of his novels.

Millais was exceptionally skilled in drawing, and his illustrations played a significant role in the popularity of Trollope's work. A celebrated image from *Framley Parsonage* (1861) represented Lucy Robarts in a dress thought to be so spectacular that it created a fashion of its own (see Figure 4). Trollope spoke of his close partnership with Millais in *An Autobiography*: 'In every figure that he drew it was his object to promote the views of the writer whose work he had undertaken to illustrate, and he never spared himself any pains in studying that work, so as to enable him to do so. I have carried on some of those characters from book to book, and have had my own early ideas impressed indelibly on my memory by the excellence of his delineations' (Chapter 8).

In *Orley Farm*, Trollope's open acknowledgement of the fictional nature of his narratives led him, unusually, to recognize and exploit the part that the illustrations played in shaping his reader's response to his characters. In recalling the unhappy Lady Mason's response to a low point in her fortunes, he refers to one of Millais's illustrations: 'In an early part of this story I have endeavoured to describe how this woman sat alone, with deep sorrow in her heart and deep thought on her mind, when she first learned what terrible things were coming on her. The idea, however, which the reader will have conceived of her as she sat there will have come to him

4. John Everett Millais's 'Was it not a lie?' (1860), an illustration from *Framley Parsonage*, shows Lucy Robarts's unhappiness as she attempts to resist Lord Lufton's courtship. Trollope objected to this dramatic image, thinking it ludicrously unrealistic, but he changed his mind when he saw a woman wearing a very similar dress.

from the skill of the artist, and not from the words of the writer. If that drawing is now near him, let him go back to it' (Chapter 63).

Here Trollope defers to Millais's image as the reader's primary means of reaching an understanding of Lady Mason's mingled culpability and heroism. Briefly, Millais becomes the leading partner in the long-standing collaboration between writer and artist. The moment is telling, though Trollope immediately goes on to reclaim his authority, informing and directing the reader's response as he describes how suffering had changed Lady Mason as she approaches her moment of trial: 'There was less of beauty, less of charm, less of softness; but in spite of all that she had gone through there was more of strength,—more of the power to resist all that this world could do to her' (Chapter 63).

Trollope valued Millais's accomplished work in providing 40 illustrations to *Orley Farm* more highly than that of any of his other artist collaborators, claiming that they were 'the best I have seen in any novel in any language' (*Autobiography*, Chapter 9). He had developed an especially warm friendship with Millais, and no doubt this personal relationship, together with the fact that Millais's prestige as an artist tended to promote his own professional status, played its part in his appreciation. Nevertheless, his tribute to Millais demonstrates the extent to which the visual and narrative cultures of the mid-Victorian period would sometimes align in his work.

On the move

Trollope's approach to story and style is formed by the persistent restlessness of his nature. Though he is often understood to be a quintessentially British writer, exploring the vicissitudes of life outside London in his Barsetshire novels or the complexities of parliamentary politics in his Palliser series, these concerns are explored in the light of his extensive experience of life outside

England. He was a dauntless traveller. Not only did he live in Ireland for almost 20 years, he began to travel abroad as soon as he could afford it. Sometimes Rose or other companions would accompany him, but he was often alone. His work for the Post Office gave him a professional reason for his more adventurous journeys, but he did not lose his appetite for overseas trips after his resignation from his work as a civil servant in 1867. He continued to travel long after most of his contemporaries would have settled for a stay-at-home life.

Even those characters who never leave British shores are often on the move in Trollope's fiction. Trollope's Post Office duties involved constant travel, and he rode up and down the land in fulfilling the responsibilities of his postings in Ireland, Scotland, and the north of England, South Wales, the Channel Islands, the South-West, London, and East Anglia. He was sometimes mapping out routes for postmen, and this gave him first-hand experience of roads, inns, and hotels across the country. In his fiction, families move between houses and modes of life which are described in confident detail, while individual men and women make momentous journeys which mark turning points in self-knowledge and may lead to growth (not always: Adolphus Crosbie, encountering Septimus Harding while on his disastrous journey to engage himself to Lady Alexandrina in *The Small House at Allington* (1864), has a flash of insight into the value of simple goodness from which he learns nothing).

The streets and squares of London are contrasted with bleak northern landscapes, or settled pastoral villages. Muddy hunting fields coexist with the comforts of well-appointed country seats. Scotland and Wales occasionally figure—Scotland usually as the location for grouse moors and hunting lodges, or grander properties like the 'somewhat desolate' Portray Castle, inherited by Lizzie Eustace in *The Eustace Diamonds* (Chapter 21). Trollope disliked Wales, and in *The New Zealander* he noted his dismay in encountering the 'strange and monstrous villages which in late

Anthony Trollope

years have sprung up on the hill-sides of Glamorganshire' (Chapter 2), built to provide homes for expanding mining communities. *Cousin Henry* (1879), an absorbing example of Trollope's many studies of weak and vacillating young men, is exceptional in Trollope's work in its distinctive Welsh setting. From first to last, readers are given a clear sense of where Trollope's characters are placed at any given point in their stories, whether in Britain or overseas, and in what kind of house or lodging. Their location is always important to the shifting perspectives of their stories. That sense of place, and of movement, is an essential feature of Trollope's complex narrative technique.

Trollope's self-effacing comments on his writing reflect the workmanlike approach that characterizes every aspect of his professional life, but they disguise the sophistication of his narrative structure and style. Throughout his ceaselessly productive career, he continues to experiment and learn. Readers are not excluded from this dynamic process. If Trollope discovers that a changing world demands an imaginatively engaged and ethically responsible level of understanding, so too do his readers.

Chapter 3
Ireland

An Irish writer

Trollope's years in Ireland were crucial to his creative identity. His
first two novels were written and set there, and he returned to
an Irish setting in *Castle Richmond*, published in 1860, shortly
after he left Ireland for England in 1859. Uncertain in tone and
narrative perspective, *Castle Richmond* deals at some length with
the famine and its distressing consequences. Like its Irish
predecessors, it met with a cool reception. Readers, as those who
published fiction knew very well, were generally reluctant to read
about events in Ireland, and they certainly had no wish to learn
more about the miseries of the famine. Trollope's first publisher,
Thomas Newby, complained to his mother that 'Irish stories are
very unpopular', and Henry Colburn (who published *The Kellys
and the O'Kellys*) repeated the point after the appearance of
Trollope's second novel: 'It is evident that readers do not like
novels on Irish subjects as well as on others' (Chapter 4).

His Irish novels brought no commercial success, but that did not
deter Trollope from returning to Irish themes throughout his later
fiction—notably in the novels which trace the political career of
Phineas Finn, that up-and-coming 'Irish Member'. Looking back
over his career in his autobiography, Trollope described Phineas's
Irishness as a 'blunder'. 'There was nothing to be gained by the

peculiarity, and there was an added difficulty in obtaining sympathy and affection for a politician belonging to a nationality whose politics are not respected in England' (Chapter 17). In practice, as Trollope goes on to concede, Phineas's identity as an Irishman did him no harm. 'In spite of this Phineas succeeded' (Chapter 17).

An Eye for an Eye, a short novel which turns on themes of seduction and violence, is the fourth of Trollope's novels predominantly set in Ireland. This bleak story owes much to the influence of the sensation novel in its reflections on innocence, oppression, and vengeance. Written in 1870, it was not published until 1879, and like its Irish predecessors was not well received. And yet the novel's treatment of tragedy and waste arising from incompatible codes of value has genuine power. R. H. Hutton, always among the shrewdest of Trollope's critics, observed in *The Spectator* that 'there is something in the atmosphere of Ireland which appears to rouse [Trollope's] imagination and give force and simplicity to his pictures of life'.

At the end of his writing life, Trollope made one last attempt to interest his readers in Irish subjects. His final novel (the unfinished *The Landleaguers*, posthumously published in 1883, with 11 of the 60 planned chapters unwritten) addressed the violent political conflict over land reform in Ireland in the late 1870s and early 1880s, and is exceptional in his oeuvre in its direct engagement with a topical issue.

Ireland mattered to Trollope's life as a writer from first to last. He was grateful for what the country had done for him, and he remained interested in Ireland's political and religious divisions and their roots in the troubled history of its people long after his return to England. In some ways, he felt closer to Ireland than he did to an England which had never seemed to be on his side in his early years. In his book on North America, he wrote that 'It has been my fate to have so close an intimacy with Ireland, that when I meet an Irishman abroad I always recognize in him more of a kinsman than I do in your Englishman. I never ask an Englishman from what county he comes, or what was his town. To Irishmen I usually put such questions, and I am generally familiar with the old haunts which they name' (Chapter 16).

Trollope's work was famously described by Nathaniel Hawthorne, in a passage that Trollope quoted in his autobiography, as 'just as English as a beef-steak' (Chapter 8). But Ireland allowed Trollope to see English life with something of an outsider's eye, and this was to his lasting benefit. Though his Irish sympathies are persistently influenced by the Englishness that formed his primary identity, as his Englishness was also inflected by his formative Irish experiences. He is now often interpreted as at least in part an Irish writer.

Irish freedoms

Why did Ireland make such a difference? One reason lay in the welcoming society that Trollope found waiting for him on his arrival. Trollope was a gregarious young man, and he took to his new opportunities for a lively social life with relish. He joined the order of freemasons (and remained a member for the rest of his life), which gave him access to the society of the local great houses. His financial troubles began to lift, and he had the money to pursue his new enthusiasm for hunting. For the first time, he was seen as someone with a measure of standing and respect, and—still more cheeringly—he found himself to be attractive to the kind of young woman that he found attractive. Ireland represented freedom, together with some degree of romantic excitement and, after some time, sexual success. 'It was altogether a very jolly life that I led in Ireland' (Chapter 4).

The headlong pace of Trollope's successful courtship of Rose Heseltine is a further reflection of the new and more confident identity that Trollope was making for himself in Ireland.

These heartening experiences found their way into his novels. The charming Phineas Finn is no intellectual giant, but his seemingly irresistible appeal to a series of intelligent women (Laura Standish, Violet Effingham, Marie Goesler) is associated with his Irishness. Though the vacuous but sexually captivating Burgo FitzGerald (Lady Glencora Palliser's first lover) is not an Irishman, his unmistakably Irish name hints at his erotic magnetism. As Roy Foster has noted, a 'debt Ireland owes to Trollope is his vision of the Irish as sexy. It is a more appealing stereotype than most, and another reason to welcome Trollope into the Irish literary canon.'

Trollope was initially based in the small rural town of Bannagher, in County Offaly (in the province of Leinster, a central region in what is now the Republic of Ireland). Bannagher was a backwater, but Trollope's experience of the country was not limited to its quiet streets. He was, as he recalls in his autobiography, 'always moving about' (Chapter 4), just as he had done in his work as a civil servant in England—travelling up and down the country in order to plan postal routes. This gave him the opportunity to learn about the country on the basis of day-to-day experience, and over the years he became better informed about its geographical layout, its communities and its tensions, than many of those who had lived in Ireland all their lives. After his marriage in 1844, Trollope and his new wife lived in Clonmel, a larger town in County Tipperary. His growing professional success and expanding knowledge of the country was inexorably leading to something other than social assurance and an increasing income. He was acquiring an interest in the political context of the forces shaping the towns and villages, big houses and dilapidated cottages, churches and chapels, farms and shops and castles that he encountered every day.

Irish politics and religion

Trollope's treatment of Irish themes and Irish characters amounted to more than the exploitation of a colourfully dramatic setting for his novels. His identity as a self-confessed 'advanced Conservative-Liberal' who was more knowledgeable and far more sympathetic in his approach to Irish questions than was usual in writers of his class and generation often led him into ambivalent and sometimes contradictory points of view, but he was consistent in his impatience with his English countrymen's refusal to take Irish issues seriously, contenting themselves instead with clichés and caricatures. Trollope does not condescend to the Irish. He was equally consistent in his scorn for absentee English landlords, who were in his view responsible for many of Ireland's troubles.

Here as elsewhere in his work he was angered by injustice, greed, and dishonesty, and he saw plenty of that in English dealings with Ireland. First-hand experience led him to argue for effective land reform. But he had no time for the Home Rule movement, which campaigned for self-government in Ireland. Home Rule is described in *The Prime Minister* as 'an absurdity from beginning to end' (Chapter 12). As an MP, Phineas Finn is a committed anti-Home Rule campaigner, determined 'to prove to his susceptible countrymen that at the present moment no curse could be laid upon them so heavy as that of having to rule themselves apart from England' (Chapter 11). In *The Landleaguers*, Trollope's implacable hostility to the agrarian rebels who had grown from the violent and inept Ribbonmen of *The Macdermots of Ballycloran* into a powerful political force shows how far he had moved from a balanced engagement with the conflicts that continued to divide Ireland in the wake of the Irish nationalist politician Charles Parnell's influence. The national identity of Ireland was no more stable than that of England, and in Trollope's view neither country was changing for the better.

Given that Trollope had made his name in representing (however ambivalently) the traditions of the Anglican church, his relatively sympathetic treatment of the Roman Catholicism he encountered in Ireland is an unexpected feature of his treatment of Irish society. Trollope never shared the increasing suspicion and hostility that marked the English response to the wave of impoverished Roman Catholic immigrants fleeing the Great Famine in the 1840s and the later establishment of a hierarchy of Catholic dioceses in England and Wales in 1850—the so-called 'papal aggression'. He knew many Irish Catholic priests, and on the whole liked and respected them. His English Catholic friends included John Henry Newman, later Cardinal Newman, who was a long-standing admirer of Trollope's fiction. The two men remained close after Newman's conversion to Catholicism (Newman's canonization in 2019 means that Trollope has become the only Victorian novelist who can count a saint among his fans).

Though Trollope was never remotely tempted to follow Newman's example and convert to Catholicism, his own religious position, which is never foregrounded in his fiction, was closer to that of comparatively high Anglicanism than that of the low church. In general he was not sympathetic to the evangelicals and 'under-bred dissenters' (as they are termed in Chapter 47 of *Castle Richmond*) who regularly appear in his novels. They did not fall within his exacting if somewhat vague definition of what it meant to be a gentleman, and for Trollope the code of values that underlay gentility was an essential qualification for a clergyman of any conviction.

And yet here too Trollope's response is divided. He was inclined to approve the older generation of Catholic priests he met in Ireland. They were, for the most part, cultivated men who had been educated on the Continent, and he saw them as invaluable advocates of wholesome moderation in the movements for radical political change that were making themselves felt in Ireland. He was much more suspicious of the new generation of curates and priests who had been trained at the seminary at Maynooth, near Dublin, an institution controversially supported with funding from the British government. These younger men were more likely to support political action to address the need for reform.

Trollope respected the solid or even fervent religious commitment he saw in many of the clergymen he knew, but he disapproved of any ambition to convert Protestants to the Roman Catholic faith. Father John Barham, the zealous priest in *The Way We Live Now* (1875), is characterized as an entirely sincere man. But his conversion to Catholicism, and his wish to persuade others to follow him, represents a kind of devotion that seemed to Trollope an abnegation of personal autonomy:

> To him it was everything that a man should believe and obey,—that he should abandon his own reason to the care of another or of others, and allow himself to be guided in all things by authority. Faith being sufficient and of itself all in all, moral conduct could be nothing to a man, except as a testimony of faith ... The dogmas of his Church were to Father Barham a real religion, and he would teach them in season and out of season. (Chapter 16)

The idea that faith could excuse immoral behaviour was anathema to Trollope. Unquestioning obedience could not be, in his view, the proper role of religion in a well-managed life.

But Father Barham is not Irish. Born into the English gentry, Barham was converted as a student at Oxford, having been influenced by the high Anglican doctrines of Tractarianism. Whether they were the sophisticated products of a European education or not, the Catholic priests that Trollope came to know in Ireland were made of different stuff, and they were generally more alert to matters of this world. Father Marty, the Irish priest, 'educated in France' (Chapter 5), who is the only friend of the isolated Mrs O'Hara and her daughter Kate in *An Eye for an Eye*, is an upright but worldly man. He is keen to see Kate make a fortunate marriage, whether with a Protestant or Catholic suitor.

Father Marty encourages a match with the eligible Fred Neville, one of Trollope's well-meaning but inexperienced and weak young men: 'He had been bred a priest from his youth upwards, and knew nothing of love; but nevertheless it was a pain to him to see a young girl, good-looking, healthy, fit to be the mother of children, pine away, unsought for, uncoupled,—as it would be a pain to see a fruit grow ripe upon the tree, and then fall and perish for the want of plucking. His philosophy was perhaps at fault, and it may be that his humanity was unrefined. But he was human to the core,—and, at any rate, unselfish' (Chapter 7). When these hopes are destroyed by Fred Neville's muddled perfidy, Father Marty becomes the moral touchstone of the story, unflinching in his condemnation of Fred's betrayal.

The Great Famine

Father Marty has little connection with the Protestant community of County Clare. But Trollope notes that during 'the days of the famine Father Marty and the Earl and the Protestant vicar had worked together in the good cause' (Chapter 5). Having lived in Ireland throughout the 1840s, Trollope was among the small handful of English writers who could write about the Great Famine from first-hand experience. *The Macdermots of Ballycloran*, relentlessly dark in its tracing of the ruin of a Catholic landowning family, was written before the famine closed in, but its focus on the poor management of the land presages Trollope's later analysis of the economic issues that made the famine so devastating. *The Kellys and the O'Kellys* was published in 1848, when the consequences of the famine were still widespread. Though this accomplished novel was upbeat in tone, and did not refer to the famine, it appeared at a time when the English reading public were reluctant to hear about Irish affairs, and its Irish setting was among the reasons for the novel's commercial failure.

It was only when Trollope had established himself in England, with several popular novels on English themes behind him, that he felt able to publish an Irish novel that addressed the famine directly. 'I might have called this "A Tale of the Famine Year in Ireland",' Trollope remarked in the concluding chapter of *Castle Richmond*. But the novel struggles to combine its accounts of suffering, starvation, and death with a conventional courtship plot, and the result is an uneasy and sometimes offensive mixture of social and political commentary and romance. Trollope's assertion that, for all the human suffering that it entailed, the famine was a necessary precondition of the modernization of Ireland's economy is disconcerting at best, and at worst repellent.

Some of the inconsistencies in Trollope's thinking are explained by his professional position. He knew Ireland well and had more respect for its people than most of his countrymen, but he was not Irish, and he was conscious of his position as an English public servant. He never doubted that it was England's right, and its duty, to take responsibility for Irish affairs—as he had done in his energetic work to improve the efficiency of postal services in Ireland. He had defended government policy in relation to the famine in a series of letters to *The Examiner* (August 1849–June 1850). In these polemical letters, Trollope is inclined to downplay the scale of the disaster, claiming that the more graphic accounts of the famine had been exaggerated. 'During the whole period of the famine I never saw a dead body lying exposed in the open air, either in a town or in the country.' He argued that the measures to deliver aid had the regrettable effect of undermining the Irish self-reliance that in his view was necessary for a prosperous future. 'Idle habits were engendered... fraud was made easy, and... last and worst, the people were taught to know that if they do not work and feed themselves, others must work and feed them.' As ever, Trollope was inclined to endorse disciplined hard work as the most reliable cure for misfortune. Nevertheless, he insists that in this emergency the intervention of the state had been essential. 'The salvation of life was the object, the ill effects were known to be unavoidable.' Here Trollope's position was an uncomfortable mix of personal conviction, human pity, and the loyalty that as a civil servant he felt that he owed to the British government.

In *Castle Richmond* he continues to praise the relief efforts of Peel's government in the early stages of the famine. 'It is in such emergencies as these that the watching and the wisdom of a government are necessary; and I shall always think—as I did think then—that the wisdom of its action and the wisdom of its abstinence from action were very good' (Chapter 31). Trollope was not oblivious to the miseries of the famine, and his unsparing descriptions of the wretchedness he had seen do not lack compassion. Nevertheless, he thought—as he remarked in the 'Conclusion' of *North America*—that 'Ireland's Famine was the punishment of her imprudence and idleness, but it has given to her prosperity and progress.'

As a firm supporter of the Union, Trollope hoped that the long-term effect of the Great Famine would be to align the culture and economy of Ireland more closely with those of England, encouraging England to recognize the particular strengths and potential of Ireland. He never swerved from his conviction that what Ireland chiefly needed were the middle-class values of exertion, enterprise, and social responsibility that had driven the growing prosperity of England. But these hopes seemed doomed to failure. His last words on Ireland, written after two visits to the country in 1882, the year of his death, signalled his growing alienation from what he conceived to be the dangerous and destructive direction that the country was taking. He was appalled by the Phoenix Park murders in Dublin, where a breakaway group of Fenians (the 'Invincibles') killed Lord Frederick Cavendish, the newly appointed Chief Secretary for Ireland, and Thomas Henry

Burke, the permanent Under-Secretary, on 6 May 1882, and this hardened his increasingly pessimistic position.

Trollope's hostility towards the Land League (formed in 1879 to campaign for tenants' rights in Ireland) and his resistance to the drive for Home Rule became more vehement. *The Landleaguers* was primarily written to protest against the Land War associated with the activities of the Land League, which were, though the League was formally opposed to violence, sometimes aggressive. Trollope was dismayed: 'There can be no doubt that Ireland has been and still is in a most precarious condition, that life has been altogether unsafe there, and that property has been jeopardised in a degree unknown for many years in the British Islands' (Chapter 41).

He was exaggerating, and the febrile tone of the novel was hardly justified by the work of the Land League, which was in fact often a conciliatory organization. But factors other than the movements of history lay behind the uncharacteristic animus of *The Landleaguers*. The Ireland that he had loved as a young man, the country that had saved his life, was disappearing, and with it his hope that Ireland and England could share a successful future. This was the greatest disappointment of Trollope's political life.

Chapter 4
Chronicling Barsetshire

An imagined county

It was the fictional world of Barsetshire that provided Trollope with his breakthrough as a writer. The glimmer of success provided by *The Warden*, despite Trollope's continuing failure to earn any significant income from his writing (fewer than 400 copies of *The Warden* had been sold six months after its publication), was partly due to dextrous treatment of the novel's narrative. The principal plot is developed alongside a network of connected stories with a skill that was to become characteristic of Trollope's mature fiction. The appeal of its central character was also significant, for the unassuming goodness of Septimus Harding as he endures his great trial is compelling.

Making virtue attractive is a difficult feat for a novelist, given that readers usually find wickedness and bad behaviour much more engaging. This is a test that Trollope triumphantly passes in *The Warden*. But the setting of the novel among the quiet cloisters and streets of the fictional Barchester, a cathedral city that was to become so familiar to the swelling numbers of Trollope's readers, is also key to the novel's seminal achievement. Barchester turned out to be a place that a wide cross-section of Trollope's market found to be of engrossing interest.

Mid-century novelists were catering for a growing readership, as the literacy, leisure, and financial resource necessary for the consumption of fiction became more widespread among an expanding middle class. Technological advances meant that books were, relatively speaking, becoming cheaper, improvements in transport led to more efficient distribution networks, and circulating libraries like the influential and popular Mudie's Lending Library were extending their reach. As gas and electric lighting became more widely available later in the century, readers no longer had to depend on the light of candles or lamps in order to read after dark. The enjoyment of fiction was a reflection of the nation's expanding prosperity.

The commercial success of a novel might depend on its being designed to reach a niche market. But a handful of novelists were able to attract readers across a broad section of the population. Charles Dickens was read by rich and poor alike, while one of the objections to the extraordinary success of the sensation novel in the early 1860s was that the thrills it provided for its eager readers seemed to challenge the ordered social hierarchies of rank and class. Ellen Wood's racy *East Lynne* (1861) was enthusiastically devoured by readers from the Prince of Wales to newly literate domestic servants.

Barchester provided a quieter location than East Lynne, but the tensions and conflicts that played themselves out within its communities proved to be equally absorbing to a new generation of readers. They reflected changing relations between men and women, between inherited privilege and wealth and the money that was being made by a rising class of commercial and industrial entrepreneurs, and the shifting cultural authority represented by the established church. Trollope was acutely aware of the advantages of constructing a fictional model that would exercise a wide appeal to male and female readers, young and old, romantic or pragmatic, representing differing levels of education, income, or social standing. The people of his imagined Barchester allowed him to explore fundamental issues in a rapidly changing society, while entertaining his readers—and, for the first time, making a significant income from his writing.

Barchester Towers

After the encouraging reception of *The Warden*, Trollope published five further novels set in Barsetshire—*Barchester Towers* (1857), *Doctor Thorne* (1858), *Framley Parsonage* (1861), *The Small House at Allington* (1864), and *The Last Chronicle of Barset* (1867). Neither he nor his readers at first thought of these novels as a connected series. It was only when *Framley Parsonage* began to appear in parts in the new *Cornhill Magazine* in 1860 that Trollope began to look at the novels, with their recurrent settings and characters, in this light. By then, the popularity of Barsetshire and its inhabitants was well established.

Barchester Towers, which builds a more substantial and complex story around the community described in *The Warden*, was the first of Trollope's works to be produced within the unrelenting discipline of a daily writing target that was to characterize the rest of his career as an author. It was in composing this novel that he began to keep careful records of his output, counting the number of pages composed every day, with a daunting goal of 40 handwritten pages a week (each page contained around 250 words, giving a weekly total of around 10,000 words). Most of *Barchester Towers* was written in railway carriages, for Trollope was at that time hard at work investigating postal routes in Ireland.

Trollope's attempts to promote the completed manuscript had unpromising beginnings. The high-minded William Longman was doubtful, noting that Joseph Cauvin, deputed to read the manuscript, had found the novel to be marred by 'vulgarity and exaggeration'. Longman was reluctant to pay £100 for the novel, and Trollope, who was beginning to feel confident in his powers as a writer, was not willing to accept less. 'It appears that you think

£100 too high a sum to pay in advance for the book. It seems to me that if a three-vol. novel be worth anything it must be worth that.' Longman eventually gave way. Trollope remembered this triumph in his autobiography: 'I received my £100, in advance, with profound delight' (Chapter 6).

Despite Longman's misgivings, *Barchester Towers* became the first of Trollope's publications to achieve real popular success. The story turns on the conflict between the reforming evangelical faction of the church, represented by Bishop Proudie together with his formidable wife, who join forces with the repellent chaplain Obadiah Slope as they contend with the traditionalist party, led by Archdeacon Grantly. Interwoven with this conflict is the romantic situation of the recently widowed Eleanor Bold, as she struggles with the misunderstandings and machinations that surround the competition of three very different suitors for her hand—including, to her dismay, Obadiah Slope. The misadventures encountered by Slope in his tireless hunt for a wife serve as a comic mirror for her difficulties.

The demanding schedule of work that went into the composition of *Barchester Towers*, and the fraught negotiations with Longman that preceded its publication, did not mean that Trollope found the production of this novel to be a burden. He recalls the process in his autobiography: 'In the writing of *Barchester Towers* I took great delight. The bishop and Mrs. Proudie were very real to me, as were also the troubles of the archdeacon and the loves of Mr. Slope' (Chapter 6). The novel's focus on the ecclesiastical society of Barchester, with its contested preferments and appointments and controversies, provided a framework that Trollope was able to develop in further novels placed around Barchester's cathedral close.

His inclination, here as elsewhere in his fiction, was to endorse the claims of traditionally minded and gentlemanly churchmen. But he does not present his readers with matters of theological doctrine, nor with the intensities of spiritual life. What interests him are the relations of men and women in a relatively enclosed community (though often with connections that extend beyond Barchester), with their differing interpretations of social responsibility, the proper exercise of power and influence, and the complications of courtship and marriage. Trollope sees the life of the clergy as a matter of professional identity, not essentially different from the civil service in which he was employed, or the legal profession that his father had unsuccessfully pursued. The Barchester novels are ecclesiastical, but they are not theological.

Trollope was now in full flow as a novelist, but his imagination was not wholly focused on Barsetshire. Once *Barchester Towers* was complete, he set about writing *The Three Clerks*, a high-spirited novel drawing on Trollope's close knowledge of the civil service, and depicting—neither for the first nor the last time—the distracting entanglements encountered by a young man attempting to establish a path into successful adulthood. Charley Tudor, the novel's inept but likeable central character, is as close an approach to an autobiographical account of Trollope's own problematic early years as he was ever to attempt. *The Three Clerks* was published in 1857, and was widely reviewed, in broadly positive terms. Trollope was steadily building a reputation as a novelist to be reckoned with—but he was still finding his way.

Doctor Thorne

His next novel, *Doctor Thorne*, published in 1858, was a lengthier and more ambitious book than *The Three Clerks*, and included many elements of the sensationalism that was beginning to make itself felt as a fashionable element within domestic fiction. Though it is set in Barsetshire and came to be included within the Barchester series, any connections with the decorous ecclesiastical society of the city are tenuous. This is a story that deals with murder and vengeance, alcoholism, illegitimacy, corrupt politics, and the ruthless pursuit of the money that might be gained by

5. This photograph of Anthony Trollope and his brother Tom, dating from the early 1860s, reflects their close but competitive relationship. Trollope commented: 'You will perceive that my brother is pitching into me. He always did.'

advantageous marriage rather than work. 'Instead of heart beating to heart in sympathetic unison, purse chinks to purse' (Chapter 21).

Doctor Thorne is unique among Trollope's novels in having a plot that did not emerge from his own fertile powers of invention. It was suggested by his brother Tom during a stay in his villa in Florence (see Figure 5). Perhaps Trollope's exceptional willingness to share the creative process at this point in his life reflects some sense of strain in sustaining a punishing rate of production, leading to a story with hectic elements that are at odds with the characteristic tone of the Barsetshire novels. But the book also reflects Trollope's growing assurance in the management of the methods and themes that sustain his mature work.

Mary Thorne, central to the novel's plot, is the illegitimate daughter of Henry Thorne, a well-to-do rogue, and Mary Scatcherd, 'apprentice to a straw-bonnet maker' (Chapter 2).

Mary Scatcherd's brother Roger is enraged by the seduction of his sister, and murders Henry. Mary leaves to make a new life in America. Her baby is left to the care of the respectable Dr Thorne, Henry's brother. She becomes a beautiful and spirited young woman, but her marriage prospects are blighted by the circumstances of her birth and lack of fortune. Trollope, here as always resistant to the sensational convention of tantalizing his readers with secrets, explains the situation from the start. The suspense arises from the uncertainties of Mary's future, not the misfortunes of her past. She has a worthy lover in Frank Gresham, heir to the Greshambury estate, but financial troubles in Frank's family mean that Frank is under intense pressure to marry money. Mary does not pass muster as a suitable bride.

One of the striking features of *Doctor Thorne* is Trollope's refusal to associate Mary's innocence with anything akin to submissive meekness. She knows her value, and in her mocking refusal to accept the superiority of the well-born Greshams Trollope signals both his sympathy for young women who are seen as commodities (valuable or otherwise) on the marriage market, and his resistance to the notion that human worth is simply a matter of inherited status. 'If I humble myself very low; if I kneel through the whole evening in a corner; if I put my neck down and let all your cousins trample on it, and then your aunt, would that not make atonement? I would not object to wearing sackcloth either; and I'd eat a little ashes—or, at any rate, I'd try' (Chapter 4). Mary is seen to deserve the happy turn of fortune that finally solves her problems—though Trollope is always careful to have his readers understand that, despite her humble origins, Mary is in every sense a lady, and that this is essential to her being the right marriage partner for Frank. Trollope's egalitarianism only goes so far.

The plot of *Doctor Thorne* may not have been entirely of Trollope's making, nor was its quasi-sensational ebullience in every way aligned with his developing direction as a writer, but these points of friction did no harm to the novel's popularity.

Trollope somewhat grudgingly conceded as much in his autobiography: 'The plot of *Doctor Thorne* is good, and I am led therefore to suppose that a good plot,—which, to my own feeling, is the most insignificant part of a tale,—is that which will most raise it or most condemn it in the public judgment' (Chapter 7).

For Trollope, a compelling story mattered less than the authenticity of fictional portraits created from a fusion of observation and imagination, in their multiple interactions with a shifting social world. He explains in *An Autobiography*:

> A novel should give a picture of common life enlivened by humour and sweetened by pathos. To make that picture worthy of attention, the canvas should be crowded with real portraits, not of individuals known to the world or to the author, but of created personages impregnated with traits of character which are known. To my thinking, the plot is but the vehicle for all this; and when you have the vehicle without the passengers, a story of mystery in which the agents never spring to life, you have but a wooden show. There must, however, be a story. You must provide a vehicle of some sort. (Chapter 7)

Doctor Thorne combined a gripping plot with engaging characters, and sold in gratifyingly large numbers. It added to the growing sense that Trollope, who was now publishing at a furious pace, had become a major presence in the literary marketplace.

Much of *Doctor Thorne* was written while Trollope was travelling, having been sent to Egypt on Post Office business. Once that manuscript was complete, he immediately began to work on his next novel—*The Bertrams* (1859), which includes many sections located overseas, with no reference to the inhabitants of Barchester. The character of Caroline Waddington, the misguided but sexually compelling heroine whose decision to pursue worldly ambition rather than emotional fulfilment is duly punished, reflects Trollope's increasing openness to different

Anthony Trollope

46

models for the lives of young women. Though Caroline is not granted a happy ending comparable with Mary Thorne's fictional reward, her wish to make decisions and seek success on her own terms is sympathetically treated.

The Bertrams did not achieve the resounding commercial success of *Doctor Thorne*. The muted conclusion of the novel, where the best that can be said of the long-delayed and childless marriage of Caroline and her suitor George Bertram was that they were 'not unhappy' (Chapter 47), lacked the satisfactions of an ending where all awkward difficulties have been cleared out of the way. Readers might also have been deterred by George's extended crisis of faith—should he, or should he not, become a clergyman? Surprisingly, *The Bertrams* had much more to say about the challenges of a religious life than any of his Barsetshire novels.

Framley Parsonage

Trollope had many other projects under way at this busy period of his life—too many to be cast down by the relative failure of *The Bertrams*. He was at work on a substantial travel book, *The West Indies and the Spanish Main*, which was also published in 1859. He was producing a stream of short stories, predominantly with reference to his experiences as a traveller. He was moving from Ireland to England, and had begun to work on *Castle Richmond*, a novel which looks back on the formative Irish phase in his life. And in 1860, in accepting an offer from the publisher George Smith for *Framley Parsonage*, the fourth of his Barsetshire novels, to feature as the lead fictional serial in the monthly *Cornhill Magazine*, he made another transformative change in his practice as a writer. It was at this point that serial publication in a journal, followed by an appearance in volume form, became his customary model for bringing his novels to the widest possible audience.

The *Cornhill* was the perfect vehicle for this move. Edited by Thackeray and established in part as a rival to Dickens's journal

All the Year Round, which had been launched in 1859 as a successor to his popular *Household Words*, it was an illustrated journal firmly aimed at an expanding middle-class market, combining lively articles on a range of edifying subjects with serialized fiction. In 1860, an issue of the *Cornhill* cost a shilling— not cheap, given that some of its rivals sold for sixpence, but manageable for a family with a little money to spend on expanding their cultural horizons. In its first year the *Cornhill* published work by Trollope, Thackeray himself, Thomas Hood, Alfred Tennyson, Emily and Charlotte Brontë (posthumously), Matthew Arnold, Elizabeth Barrett Browning, and John Ruskin.

Thackeray drafted a pitch to prospective contributors that emphasized the intended diversity of the journal's audience. The readership of the *Cornhill*, he explained, would not be defined by 'rank, age, and sex', but would welcome 'a professor ever so learned, a curate in his country retirement, an artisan after work-hours, a school-master or mistress when the children have gone home . . . a Geologist, Engineer, Manufacturer . . . [,] Lawyer, Chemist—what you please'. The only qualification would be that they would all be 'glad to be addressed by well-educated men and women'. In practice, most of the readers of the *Cornhill* were city-dwellers rather than country curates, and many would buy the journal in railway station bookstalls as they travelled to their businesses. Eager for self-improvement and still more eager for entertainment, they were just the audience that Trollope wanted to reach.

Framley Parsonage returns to the ecclesiastical setting, interwoven with the complications of courtship, that had characterized the first two Barsetshire novels. Mark Robarts is a naive but good-hearted young vicar with a fondness for hunting, and with aspiring social ambitions that nearly prove to be his undoing. Lucy, his sister, is courted by the young Lord Lufton, and like Mary Thorne finds her marriage prospects threatened by the unbending prejudices of her lover's grand family. Other courtship plots involve the rival ambitions of Mrs Proudie and Mrs Grantly, colourful characters from the world of Barchester Cathedral, who had become familiar from their earlier appearances in the Barsetshire novels. 'There was much Church, but more love-making,' as Trollope remarked in his autobiography (Chapter 8). The story moves at a brisk pace, with companionable authorial comments—'It is no doubt very wrong to long after a naughty thing. But nevertheless we all do so' (Chapter 4)—and a pleasing resolution involving more than one marriage.

Framley Parsonage continues the exploration of diverse forms of womanhood that characterizes Trollope's fiction. The prodigiously wealthy and loud-voiced Miss Dunstable (whose money derives from the patented 'Oil of Lebanon') exhibits a kindly and irreverent spirit that absolves her from any charge of vulgarity; Griselda Grantly is cold and calculating; Mrs Proudie is overbearing; Lady Lufton is snobbish but not heartless; Lucy Robarts is modest and yet immovably firm-minded. The male characters also represent what Trollope describes in his autobiography as various 'traits of character which are known' (Chapter 7). Lord Dumbello is a notable example of a dim-witted aristocrat—'muteness was his most eloquent mode of expression' (Chapter 11)—and the unwary Mark Robarts's near-calamitous seduction by fashionable society is powerfully drawn. But the real life of the novel is to be found in its women.

Framley Parsonage was given the lead position in the *Cornhill*, which quickly became a hugely successful publication. The first issue sold 120,000 copies, with roughly half a million readers. This massively extended Trollope's readership. His novel proved to be popular, and played a major role in the impact created by the magazine's launch. Elizabeth Gaskell spoke for many: 'I wish Trollope would go on writing *Framley Parsonage* for ever. I don't see any reason why it should come to an end.' Trollope's days of obscurity were over, and he now commanded the heights of a thriving literary marketplace. His vividly imagined Barsetshire had taken him to the threshold of what would be the most productive and best-rewarded decade of his career.

Looking back on the composition of *Framley Parsonage* in his autobiography, Trollope recalled the detailed sense of place that had framed his Barsetshire novels. 'As I wrote it I became more closely acquainted than ever with the new shire which I had added to the English counties. I had it all in my mind,—its roads and railroads, its towns and parishes, its members of Parliament, and the different hunts which rode over it. I knew all the great lords and their castles, the squires and their parks, the rectors and their churches' (Chapter 8). Here the association between his professional life in the Post Office, diligently travelling to explore the operation of postal routes, and his creative life as a novelist, is clear. Trollope travelled in his mind as a writer, just as he had learned to travel and observe as a civil servant. His sense of affectionate intimacy with the 'dear county' (Chapter 8) communicated itself to his readers.

Even the notoriously acerbic journal *The Saturday Review*, not usually among Trollope's critical friends, was won over: 'We feel as if we had met Lady Lufton at a country house, admired Lord Dumbello at a ball, and seen Mrs Proudie at an episcopal evening party.' Readers knew, of course, that Trollope's characters were fictional, but they often referred to them as if they were not (they still do). The sense of 'common life' created by Trollope's fiction, that absorbing illusion that the novels were describing the lives of real people living in the real world, was essential to their appeal.

The Small House at Allington

Given the success of *Framley Parsonage*, it might have been expected that Trollope would have immediately moved on to another novel set in Barsetshire. But he had many other writing projects on his mind—a major novel in *Orley Farm*, which began to appear in 1861, a stream of short stories, and a substantial book resulting from his travels in America (*North America*, published in 1862). It was not until 1862 that he began his fifth Barsetshire novel—*The Small House at Allington*, which was also serially published in the *Cornhill*, before appearing as a book in 1864.

This was another success. Lily Dale, lively and attractive, becomes engaged to Adolphus Crosbie, who is sexually magnetic, callous, and driven by ambition. He breaks the engagement in order to marry the vapid Lady Alexandrina Courcy. Lily has another suitor in Johnny Eames, as faithful as Crosbie was faithless. But she cannot forget her first love (as is often the case with Trollope's women), and refuses Johnny's repeated proposals. Like the heartbroken Lily, Johnny never swerves from his commitment, and chooses a single life. Meanwhile, Lily's sister Bell becomes the wife of James Crofts, a young doctor she has loved for many years, firmly resisting the wish of her wealthy uncle that she should instead marry his nephew. Crosbie's dishonourable marriage, miserable from the start, rapidly leads to separation, and he also remains unmarried.

This is not a tragic novel. No one comes to utter shipwreck, as high expectation settles into sober compromise. The story of Crosbie's treachery and its bleak consequences is compelling, but it lacks the high-spirited buoyancy of much of the earlier fiction set in Barsetshire, as Trollope ponders the price of the loyalty that he valued so highly. How far is it right to be prepared to change, abandoning old commitments for new prospects? This is a question that reaches beyond the frustrations or fulfilments of marriage plots. Trollope knew that change was inevitable, and necessary. In his career as a civil servant, he had instigated far-reaching reforms in the interests of a Post Office that would answer the needs of a rapidly developing economy efficiently and reliably. In political terms, his self-proclaimed identity as an 'advanced Conservative-Liberal' rested on a belief in the benefits that progress would bring.

And yet the emotional register of his writing laments what is lost through change. He is wary of shifts in the relations between men and women, or between the established ranks and classes of British society. This long-standing and deep-seated tension often provides the motive power of his plots, as it does in *The Small House at Allington*. It would have been better for Lily Dale and Johnny Eames if they had been able to set aside their first allegiances. But Trollope's recognition of the need for change always coexists with his devotion to the values of the past, and he is deeply sympathetic to their inability to move on.

The Last Chronicle of Barset

There was another pause before Trollope returned to Barsetshire, as he continued to extend his range as a writer with further short stories reflecting his experiences as a traveller overseas and in Britain, together with a number of complex novels challenging cultural orthodoxies around class and gender—including *Miss Mackenzie* (1865) and *The Claverings* (written in 1864, but with a serial publication that was not completed until 1867). In *Can You Forgive Her?*, which began to appear in 1864, he started to develop the characters of Plantagenet and Glencora Palliser, central characters in the political Palliser novels that were to follow his Barsetshire series. He was also publishing substantial quantities of non-fictional journalism at this hugely productive point in his career. It was not until 1866 that he began the serial publication of *The Last Chronicle of Barset* in sixpenny weekly parts (an experimental model of publication for him), with a title that emphatically signalled to his readers that they were to hear no more of this fictional county.

Among Trollope's torrent of publications in the mid-1860s was his mildly controversial *Clergymen of the Church of England*, published in the *Pall Mall Gazette* (1865–6), a series of quasi-satirical essays on the various clerical roles within the Anglican church. Ecclesiastical affairs were much on his mind, and in *The Last Chronicle of Barset* he returns to the complex social structures surrounding Barchester Cathedral. His essays had been largely humorous in tone, but he was sharply critical of the way in which Anglican curates, often subsisting on very small incomes, were treated.

Here, as often in Trollope's judgement, the issue is primarily one of the moral value of work. Curates were not paid according to the worth of their labour. 'It is notorious that a rector in the Church of England, in possession of, let us say, a living of a thousand a year, shall employ a curate at seventy pounds a year, that the curate shall do three-fourths or more of the work of the parish, that he shall remain in that position for twenty years, taking one-fourteenth of the wages and doing three-fourths of the work, and that nobody shall think the rector is wrong or the curate ill-used!'

Josiah Crawley, Perpetual Curate of Hogglestock (an ominous job title), has been struggling to lead the life of a gentleman, and educate his three children, on a stipend of £130 a year. The family is wretchedly poor, and when Crawley is accused of misappropriating a cheque for £20 many are quick to assume his guilt. Crawley himself, his mind almost overturned by bitterness, pride, and distress, is not entirely certain of his own innocence, for he cannot account for the cheque. A love interest is supplied by Major Henry Grantly, the son of Archdeacon Grantly, who is determined to marry Grace, Crawley's eldest daughter, in the face of his father's indignant opposition—for who would want their family to be associated with an impoverished criminal?

Most readers were already familiar with Archdeacon Grantly, and with many of the other characters of the novel—Bishop Proudie and his domineering wife, Mr Harding, Dean Arabin and his wife, Mark Robarts, Lady Lufton, Johnny Eames, Adolphus Crosbie, and Lily Dale. Josiah Crawley made his first appearance in *Framley Parsonage* as a 'strict, stern, unpleasant man'

(Chapter 14), worn by work and poverty, but upright, gentlemanly, and a scholar. His character acquires new depth in *The Last Chronicle of Barset*. The story is dominated by Trollope's compelling account of Crawley's bewildered misery and baffled pride in the face of shame and disgrace.

One reason for the intensity of Trollope's treatment of his predicament is that he is recalling the story of his own father, whose financial failure brought him to the brink of mental breakdown. Trollope's balanced sympathy and exasperation as he traces the course of Crawley's distress and describes the overwhelming relief for him and his family when the mystery is resolved is among the most memorable achievements of the Barsetshire series. His personal investment lies behind the claim in his autobiography that *The Last Chronicle of Barset* is 'the best novel I have written' (Chapter 15). In concluding the story of Josiah Crawley, he makes his peace with the memory of his troubled father.

Other stories are concluded in this valedictory novel. Mr Harding's quiet decline and death, surrounded by his loving family, is contrasted with the abrupt demise of Mrs Proudie, who dies standing, with her eyes open. Trollope was later to claim that he removed her from the novel in response to overhearing members of the Athenaeum Club describe her as tiresome—though the story survives in a number of contradictory versions and may well be an invention. The love story of Lily Dale, Johnny Eames, and Adolphus Crosbie reaches its thwarted conclusion. Archdeacon Grantly is brought up against the limits of parental power, as is Lady Lufton, and both learn valuable lessons about the humility that should accompany ageing.

The novel's final words are elegiac: 'But to me Barset has been a real county, and its city a real city, and the spires and towers have been before my eyes, and the voices of the people are known to my ears, and the pavement of the city ways are familiar to my footsteps. To them all I now say farewell' (Chapter 84). Many readers have shared the novelist Margaret Oliphant's melancholy response: 'We were in no hurry to be done with our old friends.' The intimate inwardness of the Barsetshire novels, alongside their reflections on broad social and cultural themes, has ensured that they remain among the most popular and widely read of Trollope's numerous books.

Chapter 5
Politics and power in the Palliser novels

A wider canvas

Trollope's novels bind disparate interests and narrative viewpoints into stories that reveal underlying associations between supposedly separate worlds. He writes about the inner life, with all its obsessions and ambiguities, and often explores psychological aberrations that drive his characters to the edge of sanity—and sometimes beyond. He traces the intimate histories of the families and communities that shape the particularities of individual personalities, particularly with reference to fractious relations between parents and children.

But he was also concerned with wider political and cultural contexts, with Britain's international identity, with broad changes in the relations between men and women and between the ranks and classes of society, and with developments in models of national authority and government. Modern critical responses, succinctly summarized by William A. Cohen, have often been primarily concerned with these wider interactions in Trollope's work: 'The novels at once psychologise politics and politicise psychology, showing the two realms mutually to allegorize, as well as substantially to interact with, each other.'

As he achieved personal and professional success, Trollope established himself as an experienced and knowledgeable man of the world. In 1867, the year in which his Barsetshire series of novels was concluded with the publication of *The Last Chronicle of Barset*, he resigned his senior post in the civil service in order to take up the editorship of *Saint Pauls Magazine*, a predominantly political journal. This was in part a preparation for his hoped-for election as a Liberal Member of Parliament—an ambition that was to come to nothing, after a bruising and futile attempt to become MP for Beverley in 1868.

His extensive travels meant that he could comment on national cultures across the globe on the basis of first-hand experience. He frequented leading London clubs (the Garrick, the Athenaeum, and the Cosmopolitan), and mixed with the intersecting communities of Whitehall, Westminster, and the English gentry (clergymen, lawyers, businessmen, squires, aristocrats). His love of hunting gave him a close knowledge of provincial towns and landscapes of rural England, adding to the knowledge of the country he had laboriously acquired in years of riding over a network of postal routes, and talking to postal workers. As he moved into his fifties, he felt fully qualified to include his views on public and political life among the central themes of his fiction (see Figures 6 and 7).

Like his fiction set in Barsetshire, Trollope's Palliser novels (also known as the Parliamentary novels) were not initially designed as a coherent series. Their central hero, Plantagenet Palliser, first appeared as an unprepossessing character in *The Small House at Allington* in 1864. He was the heir of the immensely rich Duke of Omnium, and dazzling privileges of wealth and rank were open to him. But Palliser had chosen to be a politician, dedicating his life to success in that field. 'He was a thin-minded, plodding, respectable man, willing to devote all his youth to work, in order that in old age he might be allowed to sit among the Councillors of the State' (Chapter 23).

Anthony Trollope

6. This photograph was taken by Napoleon Sarony in New York City in 1868. Sarony was a celebrated photographer, but Trollope disliked him—'a horrid little Silenus'.

7. The Athenaeum Club, Pall Mall (1830). Charles Dickens and William Makepeace Thackeray were also members.

As always, 'work' is a key term here. Trollope never entirely withholds approval of those who choose to work. Despite a number of more or less endearing eccentricities (including his unquenchable enthusiasm for the introduction of decimal currency), Palliser represents a balanced and principled political position that makes him the focus of Trollope's analysis of the political condition of his country. He explains in his *An Autobiography*: 'As I was debarred from expressing my opinions in the House of Commons, I took this method of declaring myself' (Chapter 17). Success as a novelist gave him a platform for a different kind of political presence.

Palliser's gentlemanly liberalism, committed to progressive reform but embedded in cultural conservatism, reflects many aspects of Trollope's own identity. Though Palliser is not a radical thinker, his thoughtful tenacity makes him a touchstone of public and personal virtue. After inheriting the dukedom, Palliser's authority grows from novel to novel, and he finally comes to reflect Trollope's unshakeable commitment to the class-inflected structures of human value that defined his understanding of society. 'I think that Plantagenet Palliser, Duke of Omnium, is a perfect gentleman,' Trollope wrote in his autobiography. 'If he be not, then I am unable to describe a gentleman' (Chapter 20).

In fact Trollope, like many of his contemporaries, found it formidably difficult to provide a precise description of what it meant to be a gentleman, or a lady. Trollope's friend John Henry Newman made the attempt in his treatise on higher education, *The Idea of a University* (1852). 'It is almost a definition of a gentleman to say he is one who never inflicts pain. This description is both refined and, as far as it goes, accurate. He is mainly occupied in merely removing the obstacles which hinder the free and unembarrassed action of those about him; and he concurs with their movements rather than takes the initiative himself.' This is an oddly passive characterization, removing the concept of gentility from a class-based identity or the exercise of class interest. Others were more emphatic in their separation of the qualities of a gentlemen from the status of high social standing—Charles Dickens, for instance, in his veneration of the blacksmith Joe Gargery's natural virtues in *Great Expectations* (1860): 'O God bless this gentle Christian man!' (Chapter 57). Elizabeth Gaskell added a regional dimension to changing views of gentility, creating in John Thornton, the mill-owning hero of *North and South* (1855), a northern gentleman forged in a meritocratic and industrial social context.

Traditional concepts of gentlemanliness had tended to remove any notion of the obligation to work from the conventional identity of a gentleman, and certainly from that of a lady, and this was among the complicating factors in Trollope's thinking on the matter. Idleness was never a quality that he could bring himself to admire, and in his inclination to value qualities of discipline and self-determination in his fictional gentlemen, he aligns himself with the values of a readership whose prosperity was more likely to be grounded in commercial and industrial enterprise than inherited wealth and privilege. Trollope's challenging family background, and his troubled education, led him to question the unthinking assumption that human worth was inseparable from the codes of behaviour that went with social class. But he never quite abandoned the notion that there was an inherent association between the exercise of power and influence and the ideals of gentility, and this is among the principles that underlie his understanding of the world of politics.

If political conflict during Trollope's lifetime was largely defined by the ebb and flow of power between the Liberal and Conservative parties (or Whigs and Tories, as Trollope was sometimes to call them), his broad political affiliations were always with the Liberals. Among his final books is a short and largely admiring biography of the Liberal statesman Lord Palmerston, published in 1882 (the year of his death), which makes his sympathies clear. As described by Trollope, Palmerston, industrious and self-denying—'nothing astonishes us more than the smallness of the periods allowed to himself by Lord Palmerston for the amusements of life' (Chapter 1)—shares many characteristics with Palliser.

Trollope's distaste for the Conservatives is reflected in the character of the opportunistic Daubeny, who is partly (though not entirely) based on Benjamin Disraeli, the foremost Conservative politician of his generation. In *The Prime Minister* (1876) Palliser describes the essence of Conservatism, as he understands it. 'The Conservative who has had any idea of the meaning of the name which he carries, wishes, I suppose, to maintain the differences and the distances which separate the highly placed from their lower brethren. He thinks that God has divided the world as he finds it divided, and that he may best do his duty by making the inferior man happy and contented in his position, teaching him that the place which he holds is his by God's ordinance' (Chapter 68).

This was close to the definition of a Conservative that Trollope outlines in *An Autobiography*: 'He thinks that the preservation of the welfare of the world depends on the maintenance of those distances between the prince and the peasant by which he finds himself to be surrounded;—and perhaps, I may add, that the duty is not unpleasant, as he feels himself to be one of the princes' (Chapter 16). Such views offended both Trollope's sense of natural justice and his unshakeable belief that serious work should and could elevate the moral and social standing of men and women. Yet Trollope, like Palliser, was no leveller.

Despite the difficulty of defining the identity of a gentleman or a lady with any precision, these categories would always represent the best of humanity in Trollope's eyes. He had no time for subversive notions of equality. Trollope believed that the Liberal

is equally aware that these distances are of divine origin, equally averse to any sudden disruption of society in quest of some Utopian blessedness;—but he is alive to the fact that these distances are day by day becoming less, and he regards this continual diminution as a series of steps towards that human millennium of which he dreams. He is even willing to help the many to ascend the ladder a little, though he knows, as they come up towards him, he must go down to meet them. What is really in his mind is,—I will not say equality, for the word is offensive, and presents to the imaginations of men ideas of communism, of ruin, and insane democracy,—but a tendency towards equality. In following that, however, he knows that he must be hemmed in by safeguards, lest he be tempted to travel too quickly; and therefore he is glad to be accompanied on his way by the repressive action of a Conservative opponent. Holding such views, I think I am guilty of no absurdity in calling myself an advanced Conservative-Liberal. (Chapter 16)

Trollope's political position may not have been absurd, but it was certainly complex, formed as it was by tentative compromise and sometimes contradiction. Critics and readers have come to recognize that he was not, as was once assumed, an obdurately conformist figure, chiefly concerned to endorse the virtues of the English middle classes. His novels reflect dissonance and tension, as he seeks to balance his advocation of progress and reform with his emotional commitment to older codes of social value.

In his autobiography, Trollope claims that he mixed his political themes with social commentary and romance in order to make them palatable to his readers: 'I was conscious that I could not make a tale pleasing chiefly, or perhaps in any part, by politics. If I write politics for my own sake, I must put in love and intrigue, social incidents, with perhaps a dash of sport, for the sake of my readers' (Chapter 17). In fact, the various romantic or sporting sub-plots of the Palliser novels are not simply narrative sweeteners—they challenge and enrich Trollope's central political concerns, providing different approaches to the questions that recur throughout the series, as they do in his oeuvre as a whole. Who is to hold power? How is it to be exercised, and on whose behalf?

Can You Forgive Her?

The Palliser novels reveal Trollope's increasingly unsettled position in relation to major social controversies of the day. Prominent among these is the debate around the social position of women, explored through the patterns of the courtship plot. *Can You Forgive Her?* (1865), the first of Trollope's Palliser novels, explores his interest in politics in alignment with his long-standing concerns with the choices of life before young men and women finding their way in a changing world. Some of the settled convictions that had shaped his earlier work no longer seemed unquestionable.

Trollope had met the American woman Kate Field in 1860, and was immediately taken by her spirited independence. She was 23 years his junior. Field, a traveller, lecturer, journalist, actor, and controversialist who never married, was far from Trollope's ideal of a well-bred young English lady. Though there is no evidence that he was unfaithful to Rose, a betrayal that would seem improbable,

Trollope clearly found Kate attractive. She was a vividly outspoken presence in his life, and she represented the qualities he had respected in his resolute mother—courage, intelligence, and a sturdy determination to make her own way. Kate's refusal to accept domestic subservience as her lot in life challenged Trollope's views on the limitations of women's place in the world, and his uneasiness is reflected in the three closely connected courtship plots that provide the structure of *Can You Forgive Her?*

Alice Vavasor had been engaged to marry her cousin George Vavasor, but his unscrupulous behaviour led to the end of the engagement. She then agrees to marry John Grey, a worthy if somewhat overbearing suitor, who expects that she will flourish as the conventional wife of a quiet country gentleman. Alice loves him, but finds the prospect of the mundane life that lies before her to be stifling. George is ambitious to succeed in public life, aiming to secure election as a Radical MP, despite the fact that he has no real political convictions. Alice finds the prospect of partnership with a politician exhilarating, and is drawn to the idea that she might find fulfilment in working by his side, devoting her labour (and her fortune) to his support. She throws over John Grey, and renews her engagement to George. He wins a by-election, but the grubby and costly process of his campaign, followed by the need to go through it all again when a General Election is called, mean that his political hopes are destined to fail.

The reader is led to understand that Alice is deluded, and that only misery could follow marriage to her embittered and increasingly violent cousin. She is not the only wilfully self-destructive character in this novel. Glencora Palliser, the wealthy heiress who has married Plantagenet Palliser, is tempted to destroy her privileged social position in order to escape the stultifying confinement of an aristocratic lady's life. She has not freed herself from her early attachment to Burgo Fitzgerald, feckless but sexually charismatic, and fantasizes about finding freedom by his side. Burgo, unlike George, is not cruel, but he is incapable of the disciplined life that

Trollope requires of a male character who is to command admiration.

Both Alice and Glencora are seen to be breaking the codes that confer value on a woman's life. And yet Trollope makes it clear that both are to be forgiven. 'What should a woman do with her life?' (Chapter 11). Trollope remained convinced that the best answer to the question was that she should marry, and become a mother, and that she should adhere to the traditional framework that supported a stable society. 'A woman's life is important to her,—as is that of a man to him,—not chiefly in regard to that which she will do with it. The chief thing for her to look to is the manner in which that something shall be done' (Chapter 11). As an answer for Alice's self-questioning, this hardly feels adequate to the roots of her unhappiness.

Glencora draws back from her prospective ruin, and Alice returns to the sheltering love of John Grey. Both are rewarded in that Palliser (enlivened by Glencora's vivacity) begins to take her happiness seriously, and Grey is persuaded to make a serene beginning on the political career that his social position makes appropriate. Glencora and Alice will, up to a point, become contented wives. But other models for women's lives question this resolution. George's sister Kate, devoted to the interests of a brother who does not share her loyalty, has urged the renewal of Alice's engagement to George. She has no wish to marry, and she knows that George's marriage would leave her with no purpose in life. 'The truth is, I'm married to George ... If George ever married, I would have nothing to do in the world;—literally nothing—nothing—nothing—nothing!' (Chapter 6). George's final disgrace and flight to America leaves her bereft and adrift.

Arabella Greenow, aunt to George, Kate, and Alice, offers a glimpse of a more positive alternative. A widow endowed with a substantial inheritance, she can make her own choices, and is sufficiently experienced to make them on her own terms.

Trollope is dismissive of Aunt Greenow in his autobiography: '...a buxom widow, who with her eyes open chooses the most scampish of two selfish suitors because he is the better looking' (Chapter 10). This is to diminish her firm-minded presence in the novel. Captain Bellfield, the man she chooses to marry, is undeniably on the make. But he is also needy, and Arabella understands that she can help him while retaining control over her own life and her own financial resources. The marriage will be good for both husband and wife.

And yet Arabella, clever and kind, is not to be included in Trollope's category of wholly admirable woman. She is too knowing, and lacks the capacity for graceful submission that marks the nature of a true lady in Trollope's eyes. However, she is clearly among the most fortunate of the novel's female characters. Trollope acknowledges the distressing plight of women who are miserably unfortunate—a young prostitute, alone and destitute on a freezing night; or George's cast-off mistress, left with no means of supporting herself. She pleads with George, echoing the central question of the novel—'what am I to do?' (Chapter 71). In her case, Trollope supplies no answer.

Phineas Finn

The serial publication of *Phineas Finn*, the second Palliser novel, began in October 1867, as Trollope began to prepare for his attempt to become the MP for Beverley. It was completed in 1869, after that attempt had ignominiously failed (the description of a corrupt parliamentary election in *Ralph the Heir* (1871) is based on this painful experience). The mechanisms of politics were very much on his mind at this point in Trollope's life. He explores their operation from the perspective of a young man whose Irishness, and modest financial circumstances, give reason for an outsider's perspective on the exercise of power in Britain. Sexually attractive if politically naive, Phineas's navigation of the politics of gender, alongside his pursuit of a parliamentary career, becomes a vehicle for Trollope's views on the operation of national politics. *Phineas Finn* is more explicitly focused on a particular political moment than *Can You Forgive Her?*, and more directly related to the history of particular policies and identifiable individuals.

The fourth Palliser novel, *Phineas Redux* (1874), completes the story of Phineas's political career (*The Eustace Diamonds*, published in 1872 as the third novel in the series, represented something of a detour). Trollope remarked in his autobiography that his two novels with Phineas at their centre are tightly connected: 'They are, in fact, but one novel, though they were brought out at a considerable interval of time and in different forms' (Chapter 17). Taken as a whole, his account of Phineas's changing fortunes amounts to a complex and detailed account of Trollope's political position, built on an enduring faith in the social progress that men of good will and capacity would eventually make possible, but qualified by a rueful and sometimes incensed commentary on the obstructive self-interest that constantly undermined the prospect of effective action. These are political novels, but they are also intensely personal.

Women were necessarily excluded from any formal part in this political process. They could not hold office, nor could they vote. Nevertheless, they play a central part in the world that Phineas is attempting to enter. The 'woman question', as it was termed at this time, was of increasing interest to Trollope, and though he was never a supporter of women's suffrage, the preoccupation with women's social position that had shaped *Can You Forgive Her?* persists throughout the Palliser novels. Phineas has a colourful romantic history. In *Phineas Finn*, he is first drawn to Lady Laura Standish, who rejects his approaches because she wishes (like Alice Vavasor) to retain the opportunity of influencing national politics.

Further parallels with the women of *Can You Forgive Her?* emerge in the fact that Lady Laura, like Kate Vavasor, is devoted to a reckless brother. Lord Chiltern possesses all of the privileges that are denied to Laura, and wastes them in gambling and drinking. She uses her money to pay off his debts, thus further limiting her scope for action. Despite her growing affection for Phineas, she marries the dour but wealthy Robert Kennedy, a Scottish MP, imagining she can repress her feelings and spend Kennedy's money to continue her life as a political hostess. This turns out to be a calamitous mistake, as is customarily the case for those who marry for money and social position in Trollope's fiction. Kennedy becomes a petty tyrant, and Laura finds herself trapped. Nor can she manage her feelings for Phineas, which are as strong as ever. She is forced to flee from her husband, finding a dreary exile in Dresden. Her tragic story is concluded in *Phineas Redux*.

Phineas soon finds himself entangled with other women—the rich heiress Violet Effingham, whose work in the world turns out to be the redemption of her childhood sweetheart Lord Chiltern, and Marie Goesler, the wealthy widow of a Viennese banker, who is desired first as a mistress and then as a wife by the elderly Duke of Omnium. Phineas's love interests are all capable, thoughtful women (in general, they are notably more intelligent than their men), with access to money and social connection.

But women's part in the political action of the novel is limited to the exercise of influence, and their necessarily peripheral role underlines Trollope's growing uneasiness with the rigid conventions defining the nature of the lives open to those with the status of ladies. Finally Phineas marries his early love, the Irish Mary Flood Jones—who is not rich, nor especially clever, nor in a position to command political influence. Meek, loving, and loyal, she represents an alternative version of womanhood. Mary will make Phineas a devoted wife, and she deserves his love. But she does not have the substance of the frustrated Lady Laura, nor the astute sophistication of Marie Goesler, nor the sharp wit of Violet Effingham. Obliquely, Trollope is making a point.

Phineas's power to attract and please extends to men, and it is the secret of his remarkable rise as a politician. The reader is led to understand that he has more than his share of Irish charm—and that he is lucky. The hapless Johnny Eames secures reputation and patronage by saving Earl Guest from a bull in *The Small House at Allington*; in a similar narrative ploy, Phineas rescues Robert Kennedy from an attack by two rather inept garrotters (there was a minor panic about the supposed rise in the incidence of garrotting in London in the early 1860s, though public hysteria on the matter subsided quickly). Violence, or the danger of violence, swirls through the action of *Phineas Finn*, associated with masculinity as clearly as frustrated ambition is associated with femininity. Lord Chiltern is a violent man, and Phineas finds himself reluctantly forced into a duel over their rivalry for the hand of Violet Effingham.

The violence of the novel is not confined to physical threat. Men are described as 'violently' in love, or 'violent' in political debate. The defining characteristics of masculinity revolve around forms of conflict, including the political contention that drives the plot of *Phineas Finn*. Phineas, the 'Irish Member', takes his place in the House of Commons in the Liberal interest. But his preoccupation with Irish affairs complicates his relations with his party. Influenced by the arguments of Joshua Monk, a Radical politician (Monk is not based on an identifiable figure in the politics of the period, though some of his ideas are comparable with those of the Radical campaigner Richard Cobden), Finn finds his commitment to reform in Ireland, and particularly to the extension of tenants' rights, is at odds with the demands of party loyalty. He is compelled to resign his post, and returns to Ireland, where he marries Mary Flood Jones and resigns himself to a quiet life as a civil servant.

The Eustace Diamonds

Before his account of Phineas's return to politics in *Phineas Redux*, Trollope published a very differently focused Palliser novel in *The Eustace Diamonds*, which he began to write in 1871. Though several characters recur—notably Plantagenet and Glencora Palliser, and the old Duke of Omnium—the focus is on the disreputable career of Lizzie Eustace, a beautiful and clever young widow who is also a shamelessly dishonest fortune-hunter, and a compulsive liar. Lizzie, determined to find a dashing new husband who will serve her interests, is equally determined to hold on to a costly diamond necklace, in the face of the Eustace family's insistence that the jewels formed part of the family estate and she should hand it back.

With a plot driven by crime and deception, *The Eustace Diamonds* owes a great deal to the popular model of the sensation novel. Parallels with William Thackeray's equally brazen anti-heroine Becky Sharp were also apparent, and much remarked on (at the time, and since). This is not a novel directly concerned with political process after the pattern of *Phineas Finn*. Nevertheless, the central themes of the Palliser series are further developed, through different perspectives. Lizzie's behaviour is entertainingly scandalous, but her circumstances go some way towards explaining her effrontery. The courage with which she pursues her schemes compels a measure of admiration, though the intrigues are oddly self-defeating, and she finally gains nothing but an unsatisfactory husband from her tireless efforts.

The fate of other female characters adds to the point. The capacity of young women to choose the course of their lives is painfully limited. Lucinda Roanoke loses her mind on the day she is to be forced to marry a brutal suitor in order to secure her social position. The gentle disposition of the governess Lucy Morris exposes her happiness to the vagaries of her lover, and though her loyalty is finally rewarded, the vulnerability of her position as an unmarried woman with no resources of her own is clear. In this context, Lizzie's outrageous machinations are seen to be understandable, if hardly commendable.

Phineas Redux

The Eustace Diamonds' concern with the manipulative abuse of power touches briefly on the position of Ireland. The ineffectual Lord Fawn is an example of the kind of exploitative absentee landlord that Trollope identifies as the source of many of Ireland's problems. Lord Fawn explains his situation to Lizzie Eustace:

'The property in Ireland is still mine, but there's no place on it.'

'Indeed!'

'There was a house, but my father allowed it to tumble down. It's in Tipperary;—not at all a desirable country to live in.'

'Oh, dear, no! Don't they murder the people?' (Chapter 8)

In *Phineas Redux*, the 'Irish Member' returns from his exile. His young wife has died in childbirth, and he finds his life in Dublin unsatisfying. 'After five years spent in the heat and full excitement of London society, life in Ireland was tame to him, and cold, and dull' (Chapter 1). After a tussle with a corrupt Conservative candidate, whose initial victory is overturned on appeal, he becomes an MP. The novel looks set to be an exploration of political culture and the processes of power. But *Phineas Redux*, like *The Eustace Diamonds*, balances its concern with politics with the thrills of the sensation novel.

The plot involves madness, an attempted murder, a successful murder, and a dramatic trial, all developed alongside the growing affection between Phineas and Marie Goesler, and their eventual marriage (leaving Lady Laura Kennedy widowed, alone, and desolate). Phineas's luck does not desert him in this novel.

Wrongly accused of killing a political rival, he is rescued by the loyalty of the friends, and rewarded by the love of Marie Goesler. 'Nobody has had better friends', as Mrs Low, one of his many female supporters, observes (Chapter 68).

But he is damaged by the experience, which has forced him to learn a hard lesson that has been essential to the education of Trollope's women since earliest childhood—that he is not in control of his own destiny. He retreats from society, and political ambition deserts him. 'Lord Chiltern told him plainly that he was weak and womanly,—or rather that he would be were he to continue to dread the faces of his fellow-creatures... "I am womanly," said Phineas. "I begin to feel it. But I can't alter my nature"' (Chapter 68).

This frankness, Trollope goes on to claim, is in fact where Phineas's true manliness is to be identified, and it is not erased by his near-collapse after the trauma of his trial. 'The reaction had overcome him, and he could not bring himself to pretend it was not so. The tears would come to his eyes, and he would shiver and shake like one struck with palsy' (Chapter 68). Artifice and affectation, 'that staring, posed, bewhiskered and bewigged deportment' (Chapter 68) that claims the privileges of a man without his proper virtues, were, as Trollope understood matters, corrupting the authentic masculine ideal. Phineas, whose emotions are genuine, is the real thing.

Phineas, as an honest man, feels that he is no longer fit for the theatre of political life. He confides in Lady Laura: 'What does it matter who sits in Parliament? The fight goes on just the same. The same falsehoods are enacted. The same mock truths are spoken. The same wrong reasons are given. The same personal motives are at work' (Chapter 68). Nevertheless, he finally resumes his place as an MP, and in the novel's 'Conclusion' it is implied that he will, after all, return to office. Like other male characters that readers are asked to admire in Trollope's fictional world, Phineas needs a 'useful task' (Chapter 80).

The Prime Minister

In the final two novels of the Palliser series, *The Prime Minister* (1876) and *The Duke's Children* (1880), Trollope returns to the career of Plantagenet Palliser. Like Phineas, Palliser finds that uncompromising honesty is hardly compatible with political success. His wealth and dedication have brought promotion. He becomes Chancellor of the Exchequer in *Can You Forgive Her?*, but to his chagrin is then compelled to move to the House of Lords when he inherits his uncle's dukedom in *Phineas Redux*, and undertakes less powerful roles as Lord Privy Seal and President of the Board of Trade. In *The Prime Minister*, he finally becomes the country's foremost politician as the leader of a coalition government. But he is dismayed by the need to compromise his principles in order to make necessary deals, and he is repelled by his wife's attempts to earn political popularity through hosting extravagant receptions and parties.

Despite Trollope's identification of Palliser as the hero of his political fiction, he concedes that he is too high-minded to be entirely effective in government. Glencora has some reason to claim that she would have been better suited to his position: 'They should have made me Prime Minister, and have let him be Chancellor of the Exchequer. I begin to see the ways of Government now. I could have done all the dirty work. I could have given away garters and ribbons, and made my bargains while giving them. I could select sleek, easy bishops who wouldn't be troublesome' (Chapter 56). Glencora is right, but for reasons that reflect no credit on the way the British Parliament manages its affairs. Government is no place for a perfect gentleman.

Palliser's uncomfortable experiences in high office are not the primary interest of *The Prime Minister*. Trollope is chiefly concerned with the career of the unscrupulous Ferdinand Lopez, a political adventurer who succeeds in winning the hand of Emily Wharton, the daughter of a wealthy lawyer. Trollope has previously explored the theme of the sexual appeal of the reckless adventurer in Glencora Palliser's dangerous affair with Burgo Fitzgerald, or Alice Vavasor's self-destructive attachment to George Vavasor. Both women are rescued by the loyal love of less glamorous but worthier partners. In *The Prime Minister*, Emily defies opposition and advice and marries Lopez, with predictably catastrophic results. Lopez, capable and courageous, has no moral centre. His social manner is that of a gentleman, but he lacks the principled substance that constitutes, in Trollope's view, the true nature of a gentleman. He is a financial speculator, whose confident wagers on the value of commodities (jute, guano, sulphur) all come to grief, along with his marriage.

Lopez is frequently identified by his detractors as a Jew, in terms that are deeply offensive to the modern reader ('a greasy Jew adventurer out of the gutter' (Chapter 15), as Emily's father contemptuously puts it). Whether Lopez is Jewish or not is never established, just as the implication that Marie Goesler is Jewish is not confirmed. But he is certainly not English, and he is not a gentleman—and this, for the spirited Emily, is essential to his appeal. She sees him as a means of rebellion, and Trollope is clear that she must learn to understand the value of what she has rejected. But the chastened Emily, who is a thorough English lady, is allowed to recover from her scathing experience, and after Lopez has finally destroyed himself she is rewarded with an appropriate second marriage. Trollope is often, though not always, inclined to allow his errant ladies to recover from their misfortunes.

The Duke's Children

The Prime Minister's somewhat bleak account of contemporary social and political tensions was not well received, as Trollope ruefully reported in his autobiography. 'It was worse spoken of by

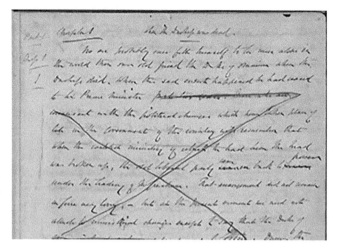

8. The manuscript of *The Duke's Children* (1880) shows the extensive cuts (amounting to almost a quarter of the text) Trollope made before the novel's first publication. An unabridged version, edited by Steven Amarnick, is now available in a World's Classics edition.

the press than any novel I had written' (Chapter 20). *The Duke's Children*, written in 1876 but published (in an abbreviated form) in 1880, found a warmer reception (see Figure 8). Trollope was approaching the end of his career as a novelist, and here he concedes primacy to a new generation. Palliser, grieving after the death of the Duchess and the fall of his coalition government, discovers that his firm-minded daughter has engaged herself to marry Frank Tregear—a committed Conservative without money or high birth—and that the match had been encouraged by Glencora. He is outraged. Mary obediently agrees that she will no longer see her lover, but she refuses to renounce him, and Palliser's attempt to impose his authority ('She must be made to obey') is finally no match for her calm determination (Chapter 24).

Palliser's two sons, Lord Silverbridge and Gerald, are equally unruly. Having been sent down from Oxford (Gerald adds to his father's woes by getting himself sent down from Cambridge), Silverbridge immerses himself in the world of racing. He finds a tawdry alternative father in Major Tifto, whose treachery eventually leads Silverbridge to lose the enormous sum of £70,000 in a reckless wager. His attempts to find a wife are no more successful. He makes a tentative attempt to propose to the polished but calculating Lady Mabel Grex, who loves Frank Tregear. Mabel sees him as an immature boy, and keeps her distance.

But Silverbridge is not among the privileged but worthless young men who saunter across the pages of Trollope's fiction. He is a rather grand version of the 'hobbledehoy'—an uncertain boy who finds the process of becoming a man to be fraught with difficulty. When he falls in love with Isabel Boncassen, a lively young American, his father is once more disappointed and upset—but this is a genuine commitment, and a sign that Silverbridge is starting to grow up. Finally Palliser is brought to understand that the choices of his children must be accepted, and in this final episode in his long fictional life Trollope's readers see that Palliser is still capable of growth.

He is rewarded by the restoration of family bonds that he acknowledges to be indispensable to his happiness. 'Now in the solitude of his life, as years were coming on him, he felt how necessary it was that he should have someone who would love him' (Chapter 66). Silverbridge, who had shifted his allegiance to the Conservatives, largely as a way of rebelling against his father, returns to his natural home with the Liberals. To complete his reintegration into the social and political world, Palliser resumes office, in a less trying role than that of Prime Minister (he becomes President of the Council in a new Liberal government).

Not every character shares in this imperfect harmony. Major Tifto, whose sordid act of betrayal had been prompted by injured pride rather than hope for gain, is left 'broken-hearted' (Chapter 58). Lady Mabel, who finds that she cannot free herself of her devotion to Frank in order to secure a suitor who can solve her feckless family's financial problems, is condemned to a life of bitterness and regret. Her tragedy, like that of Lady Laura Kennedy in *Phineas Redux*, haunts the conclusion of the novel.

Politics, in the Palliser novels as elsewhere in Trollope's fiction, is not simply a matter of elections, speeches, and Cabinet appointments, and the murky business of governing a country. It is essentially concerned with the acquisition and exercise of power, and it drives the dynamics of families, and the relations between men and women. There are winners and losers, and Trollope is unflinching in his acknowledgement of the defeat that accompanies gain. *The Duke's Children* is an optimistic novel, but Trollope's generous imagination always has a place for those who cannot be included in the sense of a happy ending.

Chapter 6
Money, inheritance, and the law

Earning a living

Trollope was persistently—almost obsessively—interested in money, and its inescapable power to shape the lives of men and women. Throughout his life as a writer, he saw the ambition to earn a solid income from his pen as an entirely legitimate and necessary motive for his labour. He explains in his down-to-earth autobiography: 'All material progress has come from man's desire to do the best he can for himself and those about him, and civilisation and Christianity itself have been made possible by such progress...it is a mistake to suppose that a man is a better man because he despises money. Few do so, and those few in doing so suffer a defect' (Chapter 6).

And yet the desire for profit was not Trollope's only motive as a writer. An unusually intimate moment in his autobiography touches on his wish for recognition and respect, an impulse rooted in the mortifications of his childhood and youth: 'I wished from the beginning to be something more than a clerk in the Post Office. To be known as somebody,—to be Anthony Trollope if it be no more,—is to me much' (Chapter 6). Writing novels was as essential to his sense of purpose, success and well-being as his public work as an influential civil servant, or his parallel life as an energetic traveller. These identities were mutually supportive. The worldly ambition that he exhibited to the world in his autobiography was fuelled by a compulsive inner life. Writing to the poet Alfred Austin in 1871, he joked that his 'only doubt as to finding a heaven for myself at last, arises from the fear that the disembodied and beatified spirits will not want novels'.

'What is there that money will not do?', as Lady Carbury remarks in Trollope's ambitious and powerfully satirical 1875 novel *The Way We Live Now* (Chapter 20). But he knew that money could not do everything. The corrosive consequences of the pursuit of money at the expense of moral or emotional integrity are a recurrent theme in his fiction. It is the central topic of *The Way We Live Now*, where the drive to secure wealth that has neither been earned nor inherited lures London's smart society to be taken in by the seductive schemes of the financier Augustus Melmotte, who turns out to be a swindler on a grand scale. Trollope wrote the novel—the longest of all his works—on his return from an extended trip to Australia and New Zealand in 1872. He was dismayed by what seemed to him a precipitous decline in the political and commercial ethics he observed in London, exemplified by financial scandals and reckless speculation. The bitterness underlying this novel, exceptional in Trollope's oeuvre, is prompted by his fear (as he put it in his autobiography) that his countrymen were being 'taught to feel that dishonesty, if it can become splendid, will cease to be abominable. If dishonesty can live in a gorgeous palace with pictures on all its walls, and gems in all its cupboards, with marble and ivory in all its corners, and can give Apician dinners, and get into Parliament, and deal in millions, then dishonesty is not disgraceful, and the man dishonest after such a fashion is not a low scoundrel' (Chapter 20).

Money was never to be despised, but it needed to be kept in its proper place. Unmoored from the values of honesty and injustice, it could consume lives, and destroy the fabric of society.

Inheritance

Trollope was hardly the first novelist to concern himself with money as a bedrock of human society, and most English writers of his generation (including Charles Dickens, Charlotte Brontë, William Thackeray, Elizabeth Gaskell) reflect an enduring awareness of its power to corrupt, or to redeem. But few were quite as careful to inform readers of the precise financial circumstances and expectations of their fictional characters. In many instances, this financial context turns on questions of inheritance, as they had in the struggles of Trollope's own family in his early years. Again, this is not a preoccupation that is confined to Trollope. In a period without the safety net of the welfare state, and where many (including middle-class women with the status of ladies) were unwilling or unable to earn their own living, an awareness that future prospects would depend on the uncertainties of inheritance was common.

Many of Trollope's plots turn on this uncertainty, which is sometimes the main focus of the story—in *Ralph the Heir*, for example, or *Is he Popenjoy?* (1878). In *Can You Forgive Her?*, George Vavasor's recklessly destructive behaviour is partly motivated by his sense that his grandfather, the Squire of Vavasor Hall, has unjustly denied him his birthright in excluding him from his will. George attempts to repair his damaged prospects by drawing on the fortune of Alice Vavasor, who has agreed to marry him but is not yet his wife. This is among the many stains on his honour. In the eyes of the law, he would have been perfectly entitled to use Alice's money after the wedding. What might be gained through a profitable match (for both men and women) is another recurrent theme in Trollope's fiction.

No one in his fictional world marries without giving some thought as to what the financial consequences will be. But those who marry, or hope to marry, purely on the grounds of these consequences are rarely permitted to thrive. Griselda Grantly, who appears in several of the Barsetshire novels, is a rare exception. She marries the tellingly named Lord Dumbello for money and social position, and flourishes. But Griselda has a heart of ice. The reader is not encouraged to see her, or her husband, as any kind of admirable model.

Issues of inheritance were not limited to the transmission of land, money, and property. Questions of inherited rank and its relations with social class were contested throughout the 19th century, and worries about what might be inherited in terms of disposition and character were also common. For these reasons, characters with no visible family antecedents are viewed with suspicion as prospective marriage partners in Trollope's fiction—sometimes, as things turn out, with good cause. Adolphus Crosbie, Lily Dale's unfaithful lover in *The Small House at Allington*, whose behaviour is in part motivated by learning that Lily will not, as he had assumed, receive a substantial inheritance, never mentions his family.

Ferdinand Lopez, Emily Wharton's unprincipled husband in *The Prime Minister*, is of mysterious origins. 'It is certainly of service to a man to know who were his grandfathers and who were his grandmothers if he entertain an ambition to move in the upper circles of society, and also of service to be able to speak of them as of persons who were themselves somebodies in their time . . . He never hesitated, blushed, or palpably laboured at concealment; but the fact remained that though a great many men and not a few women knew Ferdinand Lopez very well, none of them knew whence he had come, or what was his family' (Chapter 1). Emily's father, implacably opposed to her commitment to Lopez, would much rather she married the well-bred Arthur Fletcher, which is what she eventually does. Arthur's family has been known to the Whartons for centuries:

There had been marriages between the two families certainly as far back as the time of Henry VII, and they were accustomed to speak, if not of alliances, at any rate of friendships, much anterior to that. As regards family, therefore, the pretensions of a Fletcher would always be held to be good by a Wharton. But this Fletcher was the very pearl of the Fletcher tribe. Though a younger brother, he had a very pleasant little fortune of his own. Though born to comfortable circumstances, he had worked so hard in his young days as to have already made for himself a name at the bar. He was a fair-haired, handsome fellow, with sharp, eager eyes, with an aquiline nose, and just that shape of mouth and chin which such men as Abel Wharton regarded as characteristic of good blood. (Chapter 15)

'Good blood' matters in Trollope's world, but in this as in other matters his authorial perspectives are ambivalent. He refuses to define what gentility means. 'Bless you, when you come to talk of a gentleman, who is to define the word? . . . I can't define a gentleman, even in my own mind', Johnny Eames remarks in *The Last Chronicle of Barset* (Chapter 24). But it is clear that it has to do with honour, courtesy, and a tacitly agreed code of social behaviour acquired in youth.

Trollope sometimes seems inclined to endorse the view that a man is more likely to become a true gentleman, or a woman a true lady, if he or she has the right forebears. And yet his novels are peopled with numerous examples of those who are born with this advantage and brought up in comfort, but lack the slightest inclination or capacity to aspire to the values of genuine gentility. Darwinian theories of evolution were changing some of the ways in which the educated elite of Trollope's generation viewed the biological dynamics of inheritance, but the idea that virtue might somehow be handed down from parent to child was long established. Trollope has not wholly abandoned this belief, but he frequently challenges its reliability.

A socially responsible aristocracy, exemplified at its best by Plantagenet Palliser, might still play its part in governing the nation. But Trollope is more inclined to believe that the vigour of rising generations would outweigh an ancient lineage. Isabel Boncassen is not disqualified for her position as a future duchess because her grandfather was a humble porter, as Palliser at first mistakenly believes. Nor has Lady Alexandrina de Courcy, the empty-headed aristocrat who becomes Adolphus Crosbie's bride, gained anything worth having from her distinguished ancestry. In general, Trollope's allegiance is given to those who are prepared to work, in whatever capacity, and this would usually rule out members of the aristocracy, who are by and large conspicuously idle. Palliser's laborious devotion to his political calling is among the ways in which he is exceptional.

One of the broader social movements that Trollope explores is the shift from the landed wealth that traditionally supported the ostentatious grandeur of the aristocracy, or the more modest affluence of the country's gentry, to the money that comes from less well-established sources, including the manufacture of new products, banking, and financial speculation. These parallel streams of wealth are not always separate. The sources of Lady Glencora's wealth are not entirely based on land—there are also coalmines, and a large estate in Glasgow, an expanding industrial city.

In *Framley Parsonage*, Martha Dunstable, fabulously rich on the proceeds of selling a popular patent medicine, buys Chaldicotes, a fine old house ('if one looks at the ancient marks about it, rather than at those of the present day, it is a place of very considerable pretension'), thwarting the old Duke of Omnium's wish to add the property to his estates (Chapter 3). Trollope thoroughly approves of the robust good sense and generosity represented by Miss Dunstable. Her purchase of the house, which had become available as a result of the self-indulgent recklessness of the owner whose family had owned it for generations, is seen to be a wholesome development.

Readers were not entirely comfortable with Trollope's insistence on identifying the financial circumstances, and the manoeuvring for financial gain, that underpin the lives of many of his characters. Many found his emphasis on money to be vulgar. Meredith White Townsend, editor of *The Spectator*, was especially disdainful of the preoccupation with wealth that marks *The Way We Live Now* (1875), observing that Trollope has 'surrounded his characters with an atmosphere of sordid baseness which prevents enjoyment like an effluvium'. His comparably open emphasis on what he had earned from his career as a novelist, a prominent topic throughout his autobiography, also made mildly embarrassing reading for those who believed that a great novelist's mind should be occupied with higher matters than the need to earn a living. Trollope's willingness to share the details of his income and his evident pride in his financial success did much to damage his reputation in the years immediately following his death, as novelists moved to establish aesthetic credentials for their art. But this aspect of his autobiography isn't just a tactless form of showing off. It reflects a deep-rooted concern in his life and work.

Fiction and the law

Trollope's ambivalence about the influence of money is a defining factor in a comparably pervasive theme in his fiction—the operations of the law and the moral standing of its practitioners. Here too divisions between virtue and vice in his characters are rarely absolute. His father's financial problems had their origins in the failure of his practice as a barrister, and (like Dickens) Trollope was not always favourably disposed towards the legal profession. Chief among his objections was his settled conviction that to be paid to defend a client whose guilt is apparent must be dishonourable.

Chaffanbrass, the highly effective but venal Old Bailey barrister who first appears in *The Three Clerks*, is in every sense a dirty man:

'His wig is never at ease upon his head, but is poked about by him, sometimes over one ear, sometimes over the other, now on the back of his head, and then on his nose; and it is impossible to say in which guise he looks most cruel, most sharp, and most intolerable. His linen is never clean, his hands never washed, and his clothes apparently never new' (Chapter 40). Specializing in the defence of the guilty, Chaffanbrass is particularly formidable in the practice of cross-examination. He leads witnesses into tangles of confusion—as he does with the bumbling John Kenneby in *Orley Farm*, who is crushed by Chaffanbrass's ruthless assault: 'I ain't fit to live with anybody else but myself' (Chapter 77). George Bertram articulates Trollope's reservations in *The Bertrams*: 'I doubt whether a practising barrister can ever really be an honest man ... They have such dirty work to do. They spend their days in making out that black is white; or, worse still, that white is black' (Chapter 5).

Chaffanbrass's final appearance, in *Phineas Redux*, presents Trollope's changing view of the legal profession. Older and more human, Chaffanbrass exercises his skill in exposing the hopeless muddle of the not over-bright Lord Fawn's testimony, and rescues Phineas from the gallows. In this novel, the fact that Chaffanbrass mistakenly suspects Phineas to be guilty does not undermine his essential role in finding a way through the legal morass that would otherwise have destroyed his client. 'What we should all wish to get at is the truth of the evidence about the murder' (Chapter 60). Trollope, moving away from his earlier scorn of legal process, cautiously begins to acknowledge the principle of advocacy that he had previously stoutly resisted.

He does so with a continuing awareness that processes of law offered significant opportunities for compelling courtroom drama. For all his reservations about the legal profession, an underlying consonance between lawyers and novelists runs through his fiction. They employ rhetoric to explore character and behaviour, appealing to the reader's or the jury's capacity for judgement.

Whether or not either practitioner can hope to reveal complete truth is always open to question.

Legal questions surrounding legacies, wills, contested inheritances, forgery, or perjury, sometimes culminating in the gripping drama of a trial, provide multiple opportunities for knitting the persistent themes of Trollope's fiction into compelling plots. Money underpins legal procedures of every description, and its changing and sometimes slippery nature interacts with codes of social value in unexpected but telling ways. In *The Way We Live Now*, Sir Roger Carbury, determined to uphold traditional practices, is committed to the long-established principle of primogeniture (the right of succession belonging to the first-born child). But if he were to follow this practice with regard to his own estate, the property would pass into the hands of the profligate gambler Sir Felix Carbury, who would undoubtedly bring it to ruin.

Sir Roger decides that 'he must throw aside that law of primogeniture that to him was so sacred' (Chapter 93). Instead, he leaves his land to Sir Felix's sister Hetta and her husband Paul Montague, who will make responsible use of their good fortune. Sir Roger is one of the few characters in that novel who is seen to represent the enduring worth of old customs, but he too is compelled to recognize the need to respond to new circumstances. The practical applications of law, like the development of literary form, or the sources and influence of money, could not be unchanging. For good or ill, they would always evolve in response to an unstable world.

Chapter 7
Women and men

The sexual impulse

Relations between men and women regularly provide the fabric of Trollope's plots and sub-plots, and the foundation of his characterization. This holds true throughout his writing. But his views on the interaction between the sexes at different points in their lives are fluid, like other major themes in his writing. From the first, they are often ambivalent, and as he grew older his thinking about gender shifts alongside the changing social values of the later 19th century. Trollope is never a revolutionary in his questioning of these norms, but he is not, as readers and critics once assumed, simply a defender of the conventional sexual codes of Victorian Britain. His position reflects, often in an especially challenging form, the tension between tradition and reform that characterized his identity as an 'advanced Conservative-Liberal'.

The roots of his ambivalence can be seen in his early experiences of the family. The contrast between his father's futile attempts to make a success of his life and his mother's determined and productive career as a writer could not have been more marked. Frances Trollope, who had reached the age of 50 before she began to publish, brought out 100 volumes before she died, including 35 novels and six travel books. She earned her son's admiration by sustaining multiple identities—as a responsible wife and mother, and a productive and socially engaged writer. Tom Trollope, Anthony's elder brother, was also astonishingly prolific. He published 60 books in all, and there was a friendly rivalry between Tom and Anthony as to who could write most. The Trollopes were a writing family. But Frances Trollope was its foundation, and her sturdy example lies behind much of Trollope's divided thinking about women and their place in the world.

A fundamental feature of Trollope's representations of both men and women is his recognition of sexual attraction as a primary motive for their behaviour. As far as young men are concerned, this is not very surprising. The hapless Johnny Eames, having drunk too much punch, is predictably though briefly overcome by Amelia Roper's wiles in *The Small House at Allington*: '"By George! how well she looked with her hair all loose," he said to himself, as he at last regained his pillow, still warm with the generous god. But now, as he thought of that night, returning on his road from Allington to Guestwick, those loose, floating locks were remembered by him with no strong feeling as to their charms' (Chapter 6).

Trollope's acknowledgement that men who are not so young might also be blown off course by passion is less foreseeable. In *Orley Farm*, it is clear that Lady Mason's sexual appeal lies behind the zeal of her most committed male defenders. Mr Furnival, her lawyer, has well-grounded suspicions of her guilt in forging the codicil to her dead husband's will, which has provided her with an inheritance which neither she nor her son could legally claim. But his feelings for Lady Mason are strong, though he is not entirely conscious of them. Nor can he recognize the pain he is giving to his neglected wife. Lady Mason is not stepping beyond the bounds of propriety in taking advantage of her captivated lawyer. But Trollope makes sure that his readers know exactly what is going on, as Furnival 'took [Lady Mason's] hand—that he might encourage her. Lady Mason let him keep her hand for a minute or so, as though she did not notice it; and yet as she turned her eyes to him it might appear that his tenderness had encouraged her' (Chapter 12).

Furnival is 55 years old, but as vulnerable as though he were still a susceptible young man. 'He had formed no idea that the woman would become his mistress. All that was as obscure before his mind's eye, as though she had been nineteen and he five-and-twenty' (Chapter 40). Sir Peregrine Orme, who is in his seventies, proposes marriage to Lady Mason, with the chivalric thought that in this way he can best protect her from the risk of ruin. But the extent of his emotional collapse after she confesses her guilt to him reveals the true depth of his attachment. He takes no further interest in life: 'He was waiting patiently, as he said, till death should come to him' (Chapter 80). Men, like women, are not always able to protect themselves from the damaging consequences of sexual hunger, and an old man may be as vulnerable as an adolescent.

Trollope's women are also influenced, or even overwhelmed, by sexual longing—sometimes in ways that are to their disadvantage. In the unhappy fate of Feemy Macdermot, the doomed heroine of Trollope's first novel, *The Macdermots of Ballycloran* (1847), the sexual power that the callous Myles Ussher wields over his strong-willed but naive lover is seen to be closely aligned with the social dominance that he commands as a man. Feemy's experience of courtship has been largely limited to fiction, and this leaves her defenceless in the face of Ussher's showy gallantry: 'she certainly did love him dearly; he had all the chief ornaments of her novel heroes—he was handsome, he carried arms, was a man of danger, and talked of deeds of courage; he wore a uniform; he rode more gracefully, talked more fluently, and seemed a more mighty personage, than any other one whom Feemy usually met' (Chapter 4). Seduced, betrayed, and pregnant, Feemy's sexual commitment leads to calamity, finally destroying her, her family, and her lover. In this early attempt at

Gothic tragedy, unconstrained passion turns out to be disastrous for all concerned.

The Irish setting of *The Macdermots of Ballycloran*, together with its unremitting gloom, led to its failure in the literary market. But it also allowed Trollope more freedom to explore sexual issues than would have been possible in a book set in the context of the English middle classes. In *An Eye for An Eye* (1879), a late novel largely set in Ireland, the comparably tragic plot turns on seduction, betrayal, and a pregnancy out of wedlock. Here too a dishonest courtship ends in all-round misery and the demise of a disloyal lover. It is a mark of Trollope's changing perspectives that in this novel the beautiful Kate O'Hara is permitted to survive her ruin, though not to flourish. These Irish narratives, with their implication that Ireland might be a place where the government of female desire is not secure, represent the more punitive aspects of Trollope's approach to sexuality. In novels set in England, with plots that are in general less sensational, universal devastation is less evident—though young women who are swept away on a tide of passion are still seen to be at risk of harm.

Lily Dale is a memorable example of what might go wrong. She is a perfect lady, but her unshakeable loyalty to the unworthy Adolphus Crosbie clearly rests on her strong sexual feelings for her glamorous lover. Early in their ill-fated relationship, Lily remarks that 'Mr. Crosbie is an Apollo; and I always look upon Apollo as the greatest—you know what—that ever lived. I mustn't say the word, because Apollo was a gentleman' (Chapter 2). The Greek god Apollo, irresistibly handsome, was notoriously unfaithful to his many mortal lovers. Lily is aware of the danger, but is powerless to resist. Other young women suffer comparable fates. In *The Prime Minister*, Emily Wharton is resolute in sticking to her engagement to the enigmatic Ferdinand Lopez, another undeserving lover who comes to grief, despite the settled opposition of her father: 'I find myself to be as much bound to

Anthony Trollope

Mr. Lopez as though I were his wife' (Chapter 13). She too undergoes sharp suffering as Lopez's dishonesty reveals itself, though her husband's self-destruction allows her a second chance of happiness. She is (like Lady Mason) an English lady, and Trollope is always reluctant to bring such women to ruin.

Sexual conformism and nonconformism

In *The Vicar of Bullhampton* (1870), Trollope makes a direct approach to the sexual politics of the period. His sympathetic treatment of Carry Brattle, a woman (not, crucially, a lady) who has been seduced, makes it clear that her miserable condition as a 'castaway' is unjust. 'And yet, how small had been her fault compared with other crimes for which men and women are forgiven speedily, even if it has been held that pardon has ever been required' (Chapter 53).

The point is reinforced in the polemical Preface which, unusually, he attached to the novel, and in his autobiography, where the Preface is quoted. *An Autobiography* urges the case for justice and compassion with regard to the treatment of women who have sex outside marriage: 'It will be admitted probably by most men who have thought upon the subject that no fault among us is punished so heavily as that fault, often so light in itself but so terrible in its consequences to the less faulty of the two offenders, by which a woman falls' (Chapter 18). Carry Brattle is allowed a partial rehabilitation in her childhood home. But she is not permitted any hope of a better life, with a husband and family of her own. Trollope's challenge to the hypocrisies of sexual morality has its limits.

That women might be hurt as a result of their sexual attachment to unworthy men is by no means a new concept. Nevertheless, despite these warnings of the dangers inherent in unconstrained passion, Trollope gives his readers numerous examples of courtship where a woman's powerful sexual feelings turn out to be the most reliable guide to her path to happy fulfilment. Carry Brattle's succumbing to sexual desire brings ruinous consequences in *The Vicar of Bullhampton*, but in the same novel Mary Lowther is seen to be mistaken in renouncing her engagement to the man she finds attractive in order to make a more prudent match with a suitor who—though a good man—does not appeal to her. Trollope tells his readers that in Mary Lowther he has

> endeavoured to describe a young woman, prompted in all her doings by a conscience wide awake, guided by principle, willing, if need be, to sacrifice herself, struggling always to keep herself from doing wrong, but yet causing infinite grief to others, and nearly bringing herself to utter shipwreck, because, for a while, she allowed herself to believe that it would be right for her to marry a man whom she did not love. (Chapter 71)

In *Can You Forgive Her?* Alice Vavasor finds George, the vicious man she has rashly agreed to marry, sexually repulsive: 'Must she submit herself to his caresses,—lie on his bosom, turn herself warmly to his kisses? "No," she said, "no,"—speaking audibly, as she walked round the room; "no;—it was not in my bargain; I never meant it"' (Chapter 37). John Grey, the man she has rejected, remains irresistible to her. When he touches her hand, 'the fibres of her body had seemed to melt within her at the touch, so that she could have fallen at his feet' (Chapter 37). Here, as is usual in Trollope's fiction, the proper sexual relation between a man and a woman depends on the man's dominance. The woman must feel him to be the stronger partner.

In *The Duke's Children*, Lady Mabel Grex is more sophisticated and experienced than Lord Silverbridge, the wealthy young man she wishes to marry, and she is very much more intelligent. She does not, as Silverbridge knows, recognize his primacy, and therefore the match cannot succeed. She admits that 'I could never feel him to be my superior. That is what a wife ought in truth to feel' (Chapter 20). Silverbridge chooses instead to marry the American Isabel Boncassen. 'He is my hero;—and not the less so because there is none higher than he among the nobles of the greatest land under the sun' (Chapter 47). Isabel's feelings for Silverbridge are influenced by his status, but they are primarily sexual. Trollope leaves his readers in no doubt that both of these young people, favoured by fortune, have made the right decision.

Trollope's fiction advocates falling in love and marrying as a woman's best chance of happiness, but the process is evidently fraught with hazard. There are several memorable examples of successful non-marital households in his novels—including the unconventional partnership between the moneyed Matilda Thoroughbung and her companion Jemima Tickle in *Mr Scarborough's Family*, with their shared taste for champagne. Questions about women's choices and their consequences invite gender-focused debate that recent critics and readers have found absorbing. In this context, attention has often turned to characters and storylines that push against the peripheries of conventionally romantic plots. In *He Knew He Was Right*, Emily's vulnerability as a married woman is set against the sturdy independence of Priscilla Stanbury, who has no intention of taking the risks involved in matrimony. She is not prepared to compromise. 'I am often cross, and I like my own way, and I have a distaste for men. I never in my life saw a man whom I wished even to make my intimate friend' (Chapter 16).

Wallachia Petrie, an American feminist who appears in *He Knew He Was Right*, is among the most outspoken of those who challenge patriarchal values in this unsettling novel. Unwavering 'in that contest which she was determined to wage against men' (Chapter 72), Wally's attachment to her friend Caroline, 'the beloved of her heart since Caroline Spalding was a very little girl' (Chapter 77), hints that Wally may be lesbian. Other female partnerships, or would-be partnerships (Kate Vavasor's attachment to her cousin Alice in *Can You Forgive Her?* is another memorable example), imply an acknowledgement of same-sex desire as a possible motive for Trollope's characters' behaviour.

Kate Flint is among those critics who have drawn readers' attention to this undercurrent in Trollope's writing, noting that it provides 'numerous examples of women and men whose behaviour and preferences are decidedly non-normative—if not downright queer, by any standard'. This recognition has helped to build a more complex and interesting picture of Trollope's domestic realism for modern audiences, approaching his work with experiences and values that differ widely from those of his first readers. Here too Trollope is more closely aligned with contemporary cultural concerns than would once have been supposed.

The lives of Trollope's women are hedged about with barriers that lead his readers to question Victorian models of femininity—but male characters, baffled and sometimes defeated by pressing difficulties over their personal and professional choices, are just as likely to diverge from what might have been expected from orthodox gendered ideals. Examples of 'non-normative' sexual identities are not confined to Trollope's women. In *The Warden*, the mild Mr Harding, who figures in the Barsetshire novels as a rare example of unqualified goodness, exhibits a quality of 'soft womanly affection' (Chapter 9) that makes him to some extent an androgynous figure.

Other major and minor characters obliquely signal homosexuality—like Mr Moffat in *Doctor Thorne*, with his 'pretty, mincing' voice (Chapter 15). These divergent characters take their place beside numerous examples of men who make self-destructive decisions, or find it difficult to make any kind of decision; men who are callous and greedy, or breathtakingly foolish; men who find it well-nigh impossible to grow up. They are often supported and sometimes rescued by long-suffering wives, mothers, sisters, or daughters, who are frequently endowed with a good deal more sense and generosity than the men in their lives. Trollope is not a single-minded advocate of the primacy of masculinity, and modern readers who are interested in the history and future of gendered relations have found much to explore in his work.

Courtship and money

The men and women who attempt to set aside the imperatives of desire in the interest of worldly considerations—financial security or social status—rarely thrive in Trollope's fictional world. The unhappy fortunes of Caroline Waddington and Laura Kennedy are prominent examples of this pattern; so too is Adolphus Crosbie's cheerless marriage in *The Small House at Allington*. But there are exceptions. Not all of Trollope's successful marriages are based on physical attraction, nor does the woman always acknowledge her husband as master. In *Miss Mackenzie*, Margaret Mackenzie, who is neither young nor vivacious, unexpectedly inherits money. She finds herself with four suitors, none very enticing, and finally chooses the decidedly unromantic John Ball—an ageing careworn widower, heavy and balding, with nine children.

Trollope claimed in his autobiography that he wrote *Miss Mackenzie* with a view to challenging the expectations of his reader and his own habits as a novelist, noting that it 'was written with a desire to prove that a novel may be produced without any love; but even in this attempt it breaks down before the conclusion' (Chapter 10). John Ball had first proposed to Margaret with a view to solving his pressing financial problems, and was refused. When he discovers that he is in fact the legitimate inheritor of Margaret's supposed fortune, he proposes again, prompted by genuine affection, and is accepted.

The resolution of the novel reverts to customary expectations in that John Ball—his dignity now reinforced by having become Sir John Ball—asserts his masculine authority in his second proposal to Margaret Mackenzie: 'Nay; I will not ask, but it shall be so. They say that the lovers who demand are ever the most successful. I make my demand. Tell me, Margaret, will you obey me?' (Chapter 20). This is familiar territory, though Sir John's attempt to be a forceful lover is a little undermined by his nervous appeal ('They say') to cultural precedent. Like many of Trollope's novels, *Miss Mackenzie* does not startle its readers with radical challenges. But it does suggest some unexpected variations on gendered norms. Though Margaret Mackenzie loses her inheritance, the illusory substance it gave to her life allowed her to grow from browbeaten timidity to a clear sense of her own worth—including, as Trollope suggests in a surprising moment, a pleasurable awareness of her body. She is in her mid-thirties, and generally viewed as long past her prime. But the new freedom that her supposed inheritance brings reminds her that she is not an old woman: 'her hand touched the outline of her cheek . . . She pulled her scarf tighter across her bosom, feeling her own form, and then she leaned forward and kissed herself in the glass' (Chapter 9).

Some of Trollope's female characters demonstrate a bracing capacity for independence. Miss Todd, who first appears in *The Bertrams* (1859) as a cheerfully independent traveller with an ample income at her command, shows no interest in marriage. She is 'intent on seeing the world, and indifferent to many of its prejudices and formal restraints' (Chapter 9). Miss Todd—perhaps modelled on the character of the Anglo-Irish activist Frances Power Cobbe—appears again in *Miss Mackenzie*, still jovial and irreverent, serving as a reminder that unmarried women need not lead forlorn lives, as long as they are well educated and are safe from financial anxiety. Miss Dunstable, who appears in the Barsetshire novels, is protected from social censure by her vast fortune. She has a similarly sunny and insouciant manner, and in

Framley Parsonage Trollope remarks that 'she was content to fight her own battle with her own weapons, feeling secure in her own strength of purpose and strength of wit' (Chapter 17). A generous supply of money makes all the difference, for both women and men.

Trollope's expanding views on gender were influenced by his travels, which led him to encounter women who challenged his views of the feminine ideal embodied in the English lady. Foremost among these was the American Kate Field, who remained resolutely single, despite Trollope's repeated attempts to persuade her to 'go & marry a husband'. But other women who were rebelling against widely held assumptions about women's roles also had an impact on his thinking. Campaigners with masculine manners, advocating for women's rights with loud aggression, are satirized in the characters of Wallachia Petrie in *He Knew He Was Right*, or Baroness Banman in *Is He Popenjoy?* They reflect a brand of assertive feminism that Trollope found repellent. Champions of women's rights may be simply self-interested, like Francesca Altifiorla in the late novel *Kept in the Dark* (1882), who turns to the American lecture circuit after her attempt to win a wealthy husband ends in failure. Again, she is heavily satirized, as she imagines that 'in one of those large Western Halls, full of gas and intelligence, she could rise to the height of her subject with tremendous eloquence' (Chapter 22).

Though Trollope has no time for hypocrisy of this kind, he is not altogether resistant to the arguments of serious feminists. Commenting on Wallachia Petrie, he notes that 'there are many such in America who have noble aspirations, good intellects, much energy, and who are by no means unworthy of friendship' (Chapter 77). His experience of American women had changed his thinking. In 'Miss Ophelia Gledd', a short story first published in 1863, Trollope gives a warmly sympathetic portrait of a gifted and down-to-earth American girl (resembling Kate Field) who, like Isabel Boncassen, is prepared to take the risk that in marrying an

English gentleman she will be accepted as a lady in English society. Trollope clearly commends her wit and courage.

Middle-class English women had less freedom. In *The Duke's Children*, Mabel Grex's description of the limitations imposed on her life as a lady carries weight:

> 'There is nothing I envy so much as the power of doing half-mad things.'
>
> 'Women can do that too.'
>
> 'But they go to the dogs. We are dreadfully restricted. If you like champagne you can have a bucketful. I am obliged to pretend that I only want a very little. You can bet thousands. I must confine myself to gloves. You can flirt with any woman you please. I must wait till somebody comes,—and put up with it if nobody does come.'
>
> (Chapter 35)

If neither husband nor money can be secured, the fate of an English lady may be a wretched one. Trollope's deep distaste for husband-hunters is a persistent theme in his fiction (Arabella Trefoil, the female predator who stalks the pages of *The American Senator* (1877), is a memorable example). But he is increasingly sympathetic to the plight of women who can find no alternative path to a fulfilled life.

Disappointing and disappointed men

Men, for all their social and cultural advantages, often show themselves to be no more successful than women when it comes to finding the right way to live. Trollope's fiction is crowded with examples of male characters who bring themselves and others to disaster, sometimes irretrievably. Their missteps often have to do with their approach to questions of work, and the choice of a profession. In *Ayala's Angel* (1880), a late novel, Frank Houston is openly disinclined to pursue anything other than a life of leisure.

He nevertheless aspires to marry Gertrude, the daughter of Sir Thomas Tringle, a wealthy financier who has made his own fortune. 'Of course he hasn't been brought up to work,' Lady Tringle remarks (Chapter 14).

Trollope isn't usually on the side of financiers, but Sir Thomas's vociferous contempt for Frank is seen to be wholly justified, and Trollope's account of Frank's approach to courting a wealthy young woman is scathing: 'He knew he was doing his duty,—just as another man does who goes forth from his pleasant home to earn his bread and win his fortune in some dry, comfortless climate, far from the delights to which he has been always accustomed. He must do his duty. He could not live always adding a hundred or two of debt to the burden already round his neck. He must do his duty. As he thought of this he praised himself mightily' (Chapter 14). In Trollope's eyes, a wife-hunter is still worse than a husband-hunter.

The process of finding work, and a wife, often baffles men who are of more worth than Frank Houston. In *The Claverings*, the well-intentioned but weak Harry Clavering resists his father's wish that he should enter the church, and embarks on a career as a civil engineer. But he lacks the capacity for dedicated work necessary for professional success. Trollope rescues him with an unexpected stroke of good fortune that makes him the heir of Clavering Park and enables him to marry his faithful lover Florence, but he is nevertheless seen as a poor specimen of manhood. He had allowed himself to become romantically entangled with Lady Ongar, who is among those women who wreck their own happiness by marrying for money and position, and is now a widow. He can only escape by treating her badly. Lady Ongar emerges as a much more engaging character than the bland Florence, but she is punished by the dreary single status to which her misguided marriage has consigned her, for she is not able to forget her love for Harry. Some mistakes cannot be put right.

And yet work, though indispensable, does not in itself produce a worthwhile life. In *The Duke's Children*, Reginald Dobbes toils as hard as any man could in the pursuit of his sporting amusements, but he is not among the workers that Trollope asks his readers to admire: 'He fished and shot and hunted during nine or ten months of the year, filling up his time as best he might with coaching polo, and pigeon-shooting. He regarded it as a great duty to keep his body in the firmest possible condition. All his eating and all his drinking was done upon a system, and he would consider himself to be guilty of weak self-indulgence were he to allow himself to break through sanitary rules. But it never occurred to him that his whole life was one of self-indulgence' (Chapter 38). Work should be undertaken for an end other than pleasure or ambition. If the lives of women are to be guided by principles of moral and emotional integrity, men too must find a sense of honourable purpose in their work. In his firm assertion of these ideals Trollope aligns himself with the ideals of his Victorian readers. But a persistent uneasiness haunts his representation of the fictional women and men who so often struggle with the demands of a gendered identity, and so often fail.

Chapter 8
Travel

A global stage

Anthony Trollope is often seen as a solidly English figure. This widely shared assumption is misleading, for he was an exceptionally adventurous traveller, and his perception of England is modified by his experiences of life elsewhere. The years he spent in Ireland gave rise to five novels, and were a lasting influence on his work. Not only did he travel regularly throughout Europe, he also visited North America four times, made two trips to Australia, and travelled in the West Indies and Central America, the Middle East, Sri Lanka (then known as Ceylon), Canada, New Zealand, South Africa, and Iceland. He took an overseas trip in almost every year after his improved professional circumstances made travel possible in his late thirties, and saw far more of the world than most men of his class and generation.

His 47 novels are predominantly set in England, but they often contain substantial sections set overseas, and they feature numerous foreign characters (including many Americans) with major or minor parts to play in his plots. This is particularly true of *The Bertrams*, which in describing George Bertram's travels in Egypt and the Holy Land often resembles an extended travelogue. Four novels are set entirely outside England—*Nina Balatka* (1867) is located in Prague; *Linda Tressel* (1868) in

Germany; *The Golden Lion of Granpère* (1872) in France; and *Harry Heathcote of Gangoil* (1874) in Australia.

Twenty-two of his 42 short stories are located overseas, and they are often based on the adventures of English men and women abroad. His first collection of stories, *Tales of All Countries*, was published in 1861, and *Tales of All Countries, Second Series* appeared in 1863. *Lotta Schmidt: And Other Stories* followed in 1867, with an international flavour that persists in the stories brought together in *Why Frau Frohmann Raised Her Prices: And Other Stories* (1882). Trollope continued to embark on arduous journeys when advancing age would have persuaded most of his contemporaries to sit comfortably at home. The historian James Anthony Froude spoke of 'old Trollope . . . banging about the world', and the phrase evokes the vigour of Trollope's indomitable approach to travel.

Trollope's work as a senior civil servant meant that some of his more extensive trips had a professional purpose, and were funded by the Post Office. But he was always determined to turn his travels, whether undertaken on behalf of his employer or not, to his advantage as a writer. They gave his fiction a broader context and added to the appeal of his writing to a readership that was not usually in a position to travel as extensively. They also provided the opportunity to produce a wide variety of non-fictional publications—*The West Indies and the Spanish Main* (1859), *North America* (1862), *Australia and New Zealand* (1873), and *South Africa* (1878), together with a high-spirited and privately printed account of his trip to Iceland: *How the 'Mastiffs' Went to Iceland* (1978).

His account of South Africa, appearing at the time of the annexation of the Transvaal and the last of the Xhosa frontier wars, when the public appetite for information was keen, received particularly favourable notice at a time when his reputation as a novelist was fading. It made a significant contribution towards restoring his profile as a writer. A series of travel pieces published in the *Pall Mall Gazette* were collected as *Travelling Sketches* (1866). In 1875, a short volume based on his second visit to Australia appeared: *The Tireless Traveller: Twenty Letters to the Liverpool Mercury, 1875*. His travel writing, varied and copious, amounts to a substantial proportion of this overall output as an author.

Trollope's expeditions were in no sense to be understood as restful recreation—far from it. He maintained his arduous writing schedule while travelling, no matter how trying the circumstances. In his autobiography, he recalls the practical arrangements that made this possible: 'When making long journeys, I have always succeeded in getting a desk put in my cabin, and this was done ready for me in the Great Britain, so that I could go to work the day after we left Liverpool. This I did; and before I reached Melbourne I had finished a story called *Lady Anna*' (Chapter 19). Henry James encountered him on a crossing from New York to London in 1875: 'the vessel overcrowded, the voyage detestable; but Trollope shut himself up in his cabin every morning for a purpose which, on the part of a distinguished writer who was also an invulnerable sailor, could only be communion with the muse. He drove his pen as steadily on the tumbling ocean as in Montague Square.' In fact Trollope was not writing a novel on this particular voyage. He was writing his autobiography, approaching the task with the kind of exacting discipline that underpinned every aspect of his life as a writer.

England and its colonies

Given that he was not in flight from his commitment to produce a daily word count, what lay behind his wish to be on the move? It was a long-standing impulse that evolved into an unbreakable habit. Perhaps his unhappy childhood meant that he always felt most at home as an outsider, watching and thinking. From the early days of his work for the Post Office, he had ridden the roads and lanes of Britain, fulfilling his professional duty of assessing postal routes, but also observing the people and communities that he passed through. They fed his imagination, and they stimulated his intellectual curiosity. As Trollope puts it in the very first page of his very first novel (*The MacDermots of Ballycloran*), 'there is a kind of gratification in seeing what one has never seen before' (Chapter 1). He wanted to know, in concrete detail, about all that he saw, and his travel books are full of facts and figures.

But they are also full of speculation and comment. If the processes of the British Post Office called for rigorous analysis, so too did the customs and practices of the foreign nations and institutions that he observed. Trollope is usually ready to share his opinion, favourable or unfavourable, on all that he saw. He was rarely able, or willing, to relinquish his faith in the principles of gentility and hard work that defined his social and cultural views, and these are the touchstones of his judgements of other national cultures.

This did not lead to a consistently nationalistic viewpoint. In August 1862, he wrote to Kate Field: 'There is much that is higher and better and greater than one's country. One is patriotic only because one is too small and too weak to be cosmopolitan.' English complacency and hypocrisy is sometimes directly targeted in his writing. In the short story 'John Bull on the Guadalquivir' (1864), a self-satisfied English gentleman mistakes the elaborate costume of a dignified Spanish nobleman for that of a showman, and thoroughly embarrasses himself. But this satirical story is exceptional. His travel writing often makes disturbing reading, as an unsettling reminder of how radically our understanding of different racial and ethnic identities, and of British colonial policies of the later decades of the 19th century, have changed since Trollope published his travel writings.

The West Indies and the Spanish Main

His troubling account of the Black people he observed in his travels in the West Indies and Central America is an example of this profound shift in what we have come to know of the history and identity of the people of the Caribbean. His mission, undertaken on behalf of the Post Office, was to renegotiate the relations between London and the local authorities in administering postal services. This was demanding enough, but Trollope managed to find time to write a detailed account of the people and institutions he saw throughout the islands he visited, and in 1859 his two-volume *The West Indies and the Spanish Main* became the first of his substantial travel books. Slavery as an institution in British possessions was abolished in 1833, but its legacies remained central to his observations.

Reflecting on the emancipated Black people of Jamaica, he thought that they did not take the fundamental value of work seriously. Though 'fitted by nature for the hardest physical work' (Chapter 4), the Black man's 'idea of emancipation was and is emancipation not from slavery but from work. To lie in the sun and eat breadfruit and yams is his idea of being free' (Chapter 6). Trollope concludes that what seemed to him a destructive misconception could only be remedied by encouraging the recruitment of cheap labour from elsewhere: 'Place the Coolie or Chinaman alongside of him, and he must work in his own defence. If he do not, he will gradually cease to have an existence' (Chapter 14).

The future of the West Indies, as Trollope saw it, lay in the mixing of races. Marriages between Black and white people would in time produce a newly vigorous and intelligent race, 'fitted by nature for their burning sun, in whose blood shall be mixed some portion of northern energy, and which shall owe its physical powers to African progenitors,—a race that shall be no more ashamed of the name of negro than we are of the name of Saxon' (Chapter 4). It was Trollope's view that the mingling of racial characteristics was to be applauded rather than feared. He had no time for notions of racial purity.

Australia and New Zealand

This desirable mixing was not always, in his judgement, possible. The notion that those who chose not to function within a culture defined by British or European principles, or were incapable of doing so, would simply cease to have a viable future recurs in *Australia and New Zealand*. He found much to approve in the enterprising lives of the settlers he met (his son Fred had begun life as a sheep farmer in 1865, which was one reason for his interest in the Antipodes), and he saw Australia as an attractive destination for ambitious migrants. He noted that 'if a working man with a working family can raise £200...I do not know that he can do better than establish himself as a farmer in Western Australia' (Vol. 1, Chapter 5). *Harry Heathcote of Gangoil* (1874), written as a Christmas book for the American market, is based on Trollope's experiences while visiting Fred, and the impetuous Harry Heathcote is modelled on the character of his son. The novel reflects Trollope's familiarity with the difficulties faced by sheep farmers in Australia, and his admiration of those with the courage and determination needed to overcome them.

But he formed a low opinion of the Indigenous people of Australia, and thought that 'the Australian black man...has to go' (Vol. 1, Chapter 4). He admired the Māori people of New Zealand, but believed that they too were inevitably doomed to disappear: 'I acknowledge that they have nearly had all the gifts which would enable us to mix with them on equal terms...But the Maoris are going' (Vol. 2, Chapter 25). This inexorable decline would, as Trollope saw the future of Australia and New Zealand, conveniently remove a troublesome problem, and clear the ground for 'our multiplying race' (Vol. 1, Chapter 1). These views, firmly expressed, make painful reading. For all the capacity for generosity and compassion reflected elsewhere in his writing, Trollope was not capable of stepping outside the limits of his experience and education to see the colonial societies he encountered in anything other than racist terms.

This position was, however, complicated by the proliferating uncertainties and questions that typically characterize his social and political thought. Despite his endorsement of the supposedly civilizing mission of colonial expansion, he was troubled by the hypocrisy that underpinned customary justifications of campaigns of violence inflicted on colonized people. As always, he believed that honesty should be the underlying principle of social relations. Acts of resistance from colonized populations could not properly be seen as murder, punishable by death. The settlers had avoided acknowledging the real motives of their behaviour. 'Looking at these internecine combats from a distance, and by the light of reason, we can hardly regard as murder,—as that horrid crime which we at home call murder,—the armed attempts which these poor people made to retain their property.' He adds that 'though we can justify the retaliations of the white conquerors,—those deeds done in retaliation which they called executions,—we cannot bring ourselves to look upon the sentences of death which they carried out as calm administrations of the law' (Vol. 2, Chapter 5). Better, in Trollope's view, to admit the radical injustice inherent in colonization, and pursue policies that would at least be consistent. 'It was our purpose to be masters of New Zealand, and to rule over those people; and therefore there must be war' (Vol. 2, Chapter 25). Colonial policies should be straightforward and honest:

> When we declare to a people, as we did to the Australian aboriginals, that they are utterly deprived by us, for our advantage, of all ancient rights, of all laws of their own, and of all property,—the road, though it be rough, is straight. The colonist may be humane, as he is to a horse,—but he is persistent. But the mixed treatment which we tried with the New Zealand natives has made the government and life among them very difficult. All that we can do is to drift through the difficulties, while they are melting. (Vol. 2, Chapter 25)

As Trollope knew, blunt statements such as this were hardly what his contemporary readers wanted to hear. They have not grown more palatable since. But it was his belief that the hard realities of colonial exploitation should be openly confessed, rather than muffled with layers of euphemism and bad faith.

In *The Fixed Period* (1882), a short work of dystopian speculative fiction published in the last year of his life, Trollope applies the ruthless thinking that he had identified beneath the pieties of colonialism to his own situation. The critic Helen Lucy Blythe has pointed to the 'spectral presences' of the Māoris in this strange late work. Trollope was very conscious that he was growing old, and that his health was failing. Like the Māoris or the Indigenous people of Australia, he would become useless. What would be the reason for his continuing existence? Set in 1980 in the fictional republic of Britannula (near New Zealand), an island which has won independence from British rule, *The Fixed Period* explores state-sanctioned euthanasia as a solution to the problems of age.

The story is told in the voice of Neverbend, the President of Britannula (his name is revealing), who advocates the introduction of an allocated term of 67 years of life for all of the island's citizens. Once the fatal age is reached, they will be compelled to kill themselves. An old man has no value. 'The good of the commonwealth,—and his own, requires that, beyond a certain age, he shall not be allowed to exist. He does not work, and he cannot enjoy living. He wastes more than his share of the necessaries of life, and becomes, on the aggregate, an intolerable burden' (Chapter 12).

Trollope was 66 when he wrote *The Fixed Period*. It is the only example of a first-person narrative in his oeuvre, and the only novel set in the future. The story is told from an intensely personal perspective, and Neverbend's arguments for compulsory euthanasia are given serious weight. But the enactment of his plan is thwarted by the forcible reimposition of British rule before the first compulsory death can take place, and the indignant President is exiled from Britannula. This ambiguous and challenging novel belatedly acknowledges the limitations of Trollope's earlier position with regard to the necessary disappearance of the Māori people, or the Indigenous people of Australia. Neverbend's coldly rational arguments cannot justify the destruction of human life. To see the publication of *The Fixed Period* as a belated act of repentance would be to overstate the case, but it does reflect changes in Trollope's viewpoint as he grew older.

North America

Trollope's account of America was in part influenced by his wish to dissociate himself from his mother's viewpoint. Frances Trollope's *Domestic Manners of the Americans* (1832) was far from complimentary in its account of what she had encountered in her years in America. Her forthright scorn for what she perceived as American arrogance, American egalitarianism, American evangelicalism, American tobacco-spitting, and much else besides, created something of a sensation on both sides of the Atlantic.

Trollope was, on the whole, much more favourably impressed by his travels in America, feeling that a natural kinship existed between English and American people. He found it easy to interact with the wealthy and educated elite of America on equal terms. The spirited young American women he met from this privileged class (notably Kate Field) were appealing to him, and his depiction of Isabel Boncassen in *The Duke's Children* is testament to his admiration. He was largely in favour of the absence of deference that he saw as a defining characteristic of American society.

In *North America*, Trollope challenges his middle-class readers' assumptions on this point: 'Have you ever realised to yourself as a fact that the porter who carries your box has not made himself inferior to you by the very act of carrying that box? If not, that is the very lesson which the man wishes to teach you' (Vol. 1, Chapter 19).

Canada, still closely tied to Britain, lacked the sturdy self-determination that had fuelled the prosperity of the great American cities: 'the Canadian towns will have no equal chance till they are actuated by that feeling of political independence which has created the growth of the towns in the United States' (Vol. 1, Chapter 6).

Trollope admired the enterprise and drive that he observed in America, but his appreciation was qualified by his feeling that poorer Americans were an uncouth lot: 'I do not like the Americans of the lower orders. I am not comfortable among them. They tread on my corns and offend me. They make daily life unpleasant. But I do respect them. I acknowledge their intelligence and personal dignity. I know that they are men and women worthy to be so called; I see that they are living as human beings in possession of reasoning facilities, and I perceive that they owe this to the progress that education has made among them' (Vol. 1, Chapter 19). In his ambivalent assessment of American society, Trollope shows himself to be aware—to some extent—of his own prejudices.

The American Civil War (1861–5) cast a long shadow over Trollope's views on America. He never had any time for the institution of slavery, which he found abhorrent, and his sympathies were firmly with the Union. On his return to Britain, he lobbied for the Unionist cause (the government persisted with its policy of neutrality to the end of the war). He reminded his audiences that the Confederacy supported slavery, which was wholly alien to British values, and that the Union's plucky army was 'Anglo-Saxon to the backbone'.

In 'The Widow's Mite', a story published in the high-minded *Good Words* in 1863, Nora Field (a clergyman's daughter) is engaged to a wealthy American, but sacrifices her ambition to assemble a fine trousseau in order to send money to English weavers suffering distress as a consequence of the cotton famine brought about by the Civil War. Trollope's sympathy did not, however, mean that he had been converted to a belief in racial equality. He remained convinced, as he was to claim in *Australia and New Zealand*, 'that the negro cannot live on equal terms with the white man, and that any land, state or district in which the negro is empowered for a while to have ascendancy over the white man by number of suffrages or other causes, will have but a woeful destiny till such a condition of things be made to cease' (Vol. 1, Chapter 4).

South Africa

These views shaped his response to South Africa, another region characterized by political tension and conflict when Trollope visited it in 1877. This was in some ways his most intrepid journey, and at 62 he was beginning to think of himself as an old man. But he had achieved a level of celebrity that meant he was able to meet provincial governors, the Prime Minister, and even the ex-President of the Transvaal, Thomas Burgers. Still eager for new experiences, and ready to pass judgement on what he saw, Trollope travelled extensively (undaunted by heat and hardship) during his stay. Though he was diligent in seeking out people who could help him to understand what was going on in the country, he found the complexities of South African politics challenging.

He had not previously favoured colonial expansion, but felt that the annexation of the Transvaal had been necessary. Yet he was wholly opposed to the possibility that the Orange Free State should also be annexed. He was favourably and very characteristically impressed by the hard work of the Black people he saw around him: 'Who can doubt but that work is the great civilizer of the world,—work and growing desire for those good things which work only will bring?' (Vol. 2, Chapter 9). He felt that South Africa was a 'a country of black men,—and not of white men. It has been so; it is so; and it will continue to be so' (Vol. 2, Chapter 17).

South Africa does not raise the prospect of the inevitable disappearance of Black people. But he believed that the expansion of white rule was unstoppable. 'The white race have gradually obtained possession of whatever land they have wanted because they have been the braver and the stronger people. Philanthropy must put up with the fact, and justice must reconcile herself to it as best she may' (Vol. 2, Chapter 2).

Nevertheless, on his return to England Trollope was outraged by the provocative British behaviour that triggered the Zulu War in 1879. In a revised edition of *South Africa*, published in 1879, he made his opposition clear: 'I have no fears myself that Natal will be overrun by hostile Zulus;—but much fear that Zululand should be overrun by hostile Britons' (Chapter 11). Despite these uncertain perspectives, with ambiguities that grew more marked as Trollope grew older, by and large his views remain embedded in the intransigent racism of the period. This caused no offence to his readers, and *South Africa* achieved notably good reviews, and strong sales figures. Without question, Trollope's lifelong impulse to travel enriched and expanded many aspects of his writing, but it did not enable him to break through all of the assumptions that corroded the thinking of British people of his class and generation.

Chapter 9
Afterlife

Which Trollope?

Trollope's standing as a novelist has fluctuated with the changing tastes and expectations of his readers. 'Each generation finds in Trollope the Trollope they wish to find,' as the editors of a lively collection of essays on the gendered politics of his fiction have pointed out. His audiences have expanded in recent years, pleasurably absorbed in the fortunes and misfortunes of his characters and engaged by the challenging ambiguities of his work in the context of their own cultural interests. Adaptations for television, radio, and stage have provided new channels for his cultural presence. Recurrent themes like money, work, politics, and gender mean that his writing often feels surprisingly modern, prompting readers to examine the grounds of their own underlying judgements and assumptions.

It is worth noting that no consensus has emerged as to what might be described as his strongest or best-loved novel. Contenders include *Barchester Towers*, *The Way We Live Now*, or *The Small House at Allington*, but there is little general agreement. The extraordinary range of his writing means that individual readers and critics find different points of interest and reward in the work, while the tensions and ambivalence that shape his fiction continue to give rise to stimulating debate as to how the novels might be approached and understood. Trollope's critical reputation has risen and fallen and risen again over the years, but his readership has proved to be loyal, and more than 200 years after his birth he remains a popular and widely admired writer.

Aestheticism, modernism, and the reaction against Trollope

Trollope's remarkable productivity never flagged during his lifetime, but sales figures for his new works, which were high in the late 1850s and 1860s, faltered in the 1870s. After his death in 1882, his standing among those who subscribed to the ideal of the aesthetically inspired 'art novel' in the final decades of the 19th century was significantly damaged by the posthumous publication of his *An Autobiography* in 1883. Trollope's brusque account of his workmanlike approach to authorship, accompanied by the details of what he had earned from each of his novels, seemed to mark his work as the philistine product of a bygone age.

He had no time for those 'who think that the man who works with his imagination should allow himself to wait till—inspiration moves him. When I have heard such doctrine preached, I have hardly been able to repress my scorn. To me it would not be more absurd if the shoemaker were to wait for inspiration, or the tallow-chandler for the divine moment of melting . . . I was once told that the surest aid to the writing of a book was a piece of cobbler's wax on my chair. I certainly believe in the cobbler's wax much more than the inspiration' (Chapter 7). Comparing the production of fiction with the business of a cobbler hardly seemed dignified to critics bent on celebrating the high art of the novelist.

The rise of modernism as a dominant artistic frame of reference in the early 20th century dealt another blow to Trollope's critical reputation. Set beside the bold innovations of James Joyce or Virginia Woolf, Trollope's domestic realism looked conservative and out of date. As the study of English literature began to find a

Anthony Trollope

114

professional footing in universities, few academics took his work seriously. And yet the appetite for his books remained strong, despite the neglect or disparagement of critics. His novels remained in print throughout the first half of the 20th century, and sold in substantial numbers. Michael Sadleir, a bibliographer and book collector who wrote a biography of Trollope, was among his dedicated admirers, and his respectful *Anthony Trollope: A Commentary* (1927) helped to restore his standing.

Writers never lost their regard for his achievement. Virginia Woolf, though a leading figure within the modernist movement, was not in the least hostile to Trollope, describing him in 1929 as a 'truth-teller' whose novels provide 'the same sort of refreshment and delight that we get from seeing something actually happen in the street below'. Here Woolf echoes George Eliot, who wrote to Trollope to express her admiration of his 'thoroughly natural everyday incidents', calling this skill 'among the subtleties of art which can hardly be appreciated except by those who have striven after the same result with conscious failure'. Practising novelists were not inclined to underestimate the skill that lay beneath Trollope's deceptively straightforward narratives.

The tide turns

The denigration of *An Autobiography* was never a universal response. Many readers found its emphasis on the dogged toil that had enabled Trollope to escape from the unhappy failures of his youth and build a life of professional and personal success to be engagingly honest, or even inspiring. Among academics, a changing understanding of Trollope's self-presentation in *An Autobiography* was central to his rehabilitation. Despite its matter-of-fact tone, *An Autobiography* reveals more about his compulsive writing process than its early critics were ready to allow. His creative energy was not entirely to do with his ambition to earn a living. It was rooted in the intensity of his imaginative experience, which had enabled him 'to live in a world altogether outside the world of my material life' since the days of his lonely boyhood. His relentless schedule of work, which approached a condition of pathological obsession, had as much to do with his inner life as his concern for his bank balance. The increasing recognition of these complexities drove a new and more sympathetic consideration of his motives as a writer.

A range of preoccupations other than those of worldly success are evident throughout *An Autobiography*, as Trollope reflected on the principles that should govern fiction, and these were increasingly acknowledged by the book's modern readers. The effective management of style, character, and plot were crucial. But he also thought it essential that writers should take their moral responsibilities seriously. Novelists were entertainers, but the ability to amuse was not enough: 'The writer of stories must please, or he will be nothing. And he must teach whether he wish to teach or no. How shall he teach lessons of virtue and at the same time make himself a delight to his readers? That sermons are not in themselves often thought to be agreeable we all know. Nor are disquisitions on moral philosophy supposed to be pleasant reading for our idle hours. But the novelist, if he have a conscience, must preach his sermons with the same purpose as the clergyman, and must have his own system of ethics' (Chapter 12).

The concept of the novelist as a preacher was still further from modernist ideals than that of the novelist as a shoemaker. But literary culture had never been wholly defined by either aestheticism or modernism, and as their authority retreated, Trollope's profile began to grow. Political turbulence and international conflict darkened the middle decades of the 20th century, and Trollope's conviction that a steady moral compass was a necessary attribute for human flourishing held a powerful appeal for many readers.

During the Second World War, the comparative stability of a fictional world built on a resolve to 'make virtue alluring and vice ugly' (Chapter 12) was particularly attractive. At a time when abstract tensions between right and wrong had taken on a terrifying reality, Trollope's intensely imagined stories of courtship, inheritance, or political difference provided a welcome alternative arena for processes of ethical judgement. They do not simply represent a world of calm safety, for episodes of murder, suicide, miserable poverty, and acute suffering are common in his fiction. Not every character finds a happy ending, and definitions of vice and virtue are never straightforward. But Trollope's fiction does reflect a steady commitment to the belief that human behaviour is always to be measured against the values of generosity, compassion, and honesty. Much in Trollope's understanding of the social world that surrounded him changed as he grew up, and then grew old, but his conviction that men and women are to be judged in the light of those values was immovable.

The Way We Live Now

In the post-war period, the division between Trollope's popularity among a general readership and neglect among academic critics began to break down. Adaptations for broadcast media accelerated this process; so too did the fact that his fiction was increasingly available in a series of affordable paperback editions. Trollope's growing appeal had many different sources. The disdain for high Victorian culture that had characterized the earlier decades of the 20th century diminished, as the legacy of the period in terms of its urban and industrial expansion attracted a more balanced critique, and it began to be more widely understood that many of the pillars of civic life in Britain had their foundations in Victorian achievement.

Trollope's analysis of the dynamics of towns and cities, country houses and London clubs, the networks of local gossip and the political scheming of national leaders, came to seem increasingly relevant to contemporary concerns. He had never been a complacent advocate of the political and economic principles that underpinned 19th-century prosperity, and his contempt for the self-interested financial greed that he believed to be gaining ground among his contemporaries seemed to many a telling and increasingly topical indictment of the consequences of unregulated capitalism.

The biting anger of *The Way We Live Now* had once consigned the book to the margins of Trollope's oeuvre. But a successful four-part television adaptation in 2001 brought the book into the public eye, and its reputation was enhanced. After the financial crash of 2008, *The Way We Live Now* attracted still more admirers, in Britain and beyond. 'It is seen as his greatest achievement,' Robert McCrum confidently claimed in a 2014 piece for the *Guardian*. Not everyone would accept McCrum's judgement, but the novel has unquestionably attracted growing levels of interest in recent years. Its new prominence in Trollope's oeuvre was evident in the BBC's 2015 list of the 100 best British novels of all time, compiled by a group of critics working outside Britain. In Trollope's two appearances on the list, *The Way We Live Now* was ranked above *Barchester Towers*.

The wide-ranging scope of *The Way We Live Now*, like its reputation, is not confined to Britain. Its satire throws the petty corruptions of England into a global perspective. The mysterious origins of Auguste Melmotte, the murky financier whose grand schemes drive the plot, are subject to speculation among the lofty social circles into which he makes his glitteringly moneyed entrance, but he is clearly not English. There are suggestions that he may be Jewish, or European, or American. No one knows for sure. His wife is certainly Bohemian. Melmotte's schemes involve an illusory railway, supposedly to run from Salt Lake City to Mexico, which is never built, and his sham investment company is based in North America.

Trollope's primary model for Melmotte may have been John Sadleir, an Irish Member of Parliament and fraudulent banker who was involved in the financing of railways. Sadleir became notorious as the 'Prince of Swindlers' before (like Melmotte) killing himself with prussic acid in 1856. Towards the conclusion of *The Way We Live Now*, Trollope implies that Melmotte may have been born as an Irishman called Melmody, with a criminal career that began in New York. This hardly matters. The point is that Melmotte embodies an international moral malaise. Trollope's ambivalent representation of Britain as the home of both ideal virtue and corrosive vice, a view that grew generally darker over the years, is grounded in his understanding that British society was shaped by its dynamic relations with other nations, in reciprocal patterns of connection that were never fixed.

These patterns are explored in detail in his travel writings, but they are by no means limited to that genre. From first to last, his fiction also places the lives of his English characters in this wider context of change. A recognition of this feature of his writing is central to the ways in which it has come to be received. Lauren Goodlad makes the point in her recent study of the Victorian geopolitical aesthetic: 'As he pivoted from quotidian provincial novels to far-flung travel writings, Trollope's mid-Victorian *oeuvre* staged productive play between perceptions of England's sovereign rootedness and its colonial cosmopolitanism.'

The dismantling of the British Empire in the 20th century led to new analyses of its colonial legacies, and Trollope's readers found that his international perspectives gave his writing layers of significance that had been overlooked by earlier generations of readers. His belief in what he saw as the opportunities represented by the British colonial project, qualified by his scepticism about Disraelian policies of expansion, provided insights into the dilemmas which had often undermined the confidence of British imperialism. At once committed to the primacy of Britain and distrustful of the underlying motives of its leaders, his work now looks a good deal less insular than readers were once inclined to assume.

Patterns of gender

As critics and readers began to reassess the complexities underlying Trollope's fiction, his treatment of the relation between the sexes became a central focus for their renewed interest. Gendered identities in the West were transformed during the 20th and 21st centuries, and the imaginative tensions generated by Trollope's explorations of the difficulties confronted by women and men as they contended with the constraints imposed by gendered codes of behaviour seemed increasingly relevant to the experience of modern readers. His fiction both confirms and questions the sexual ideologies of his day. Marriage (though not always of a kind to satisfy expectations of conventional romantic fulfilment) usually plays a central part in resolving these problems. But Trollope paid careful attention to the possibility that women might refuse this resolution, as in the case of Lily Dale's resolute rejection of Johnny Eames's dogged courtship—a rejection that Trollope maintained in the face of much vexation among his readers, who wanted the lively and likeable Lily to find happiness.

Questioning patterns are repeated with variations throughout Trollope's fiction, as he tests the assumptions of the courtship plot that remains the bedrock of his fictional practice. In *Lady Anna*, the nobly born Anna stands by her commitment to marry Daniel Thwaite, a radical tailor, in the face of formidable opposition. Her loyal resolution is seen to be admirable—but Daniel's dour nature, coupled with his uncompromising insistence on retaining control of Anna's money, doesn't bode entirely well for her happiness with her husband in their new life in Australia. Once married, a loyal wife was exposed to the consequences of her husband's behaviour, or misbehaviour. She might be able to influence her husband (as Mrs Grantly does), but she is often unable to do much to protect herself from his folly, corruption, or cruelty. In *The Claverings*, relations between Sir Hugh Clavering and his hapless wife Hermione provide a devastating example of emotional abuse

Anthony Trollope

within marriage. For all her intelligence and spirit, in *Phineas Redux* Laura Kennedy can only escape her despotic husband by a flight that wrecks her life. She is only partly rescued by her husband's death. If marriage was a danger, the motherhood that followed could be fatal. In *Phineas Finn*, Phineas marries Mary Flood Jones, his Irish sweetheart. In the opening pages of *Phineas Redux*, readers learn that Mary died in childbirth just a year after the wedding.

Trollope never lost his belief that marriage was the most fitting destiny for both men and women, and he is in some respects a stalwart defender of traditional relations between the sexes. And yet searching examples of women's oppression and suffering and of the confused struggles of men who fail to live up to what might be expected of them proliferate throughout his fiction. Nowhere is the ambivalence that deepens the significance of Trollope's fiction more marked than in his thoughtful representations of the socially constructed identities of men and women and the diverse interactions that confirm or undermine those identities, with all their potential to produce contentment or misery, and nothing has generated more continuing scrutiny and debate among his recent critics and readers. This swelling tide of discussion shows no sign of receding, and it has become a major reason for his enduring popularity.

Politics and style

Perceptions of Trollope's political identity have also shifted in recent years. Here too his ambivalence as an 'advanced Conservative-Liberal' has created space for contested interpretations, as interest has grown in the ambiguities of his position. For some readers, tellingly represented by the Conservative politicians who are enthusiastic advocates of his novels (the former British prime ministers John Major and Harold Macmillan are notable examples), Trollope is an affirmation of conservative values. Others find that he exposes the inadequacy of those values. Interest in the historical basis of the specific political events, parties, and individuals that to some extent form the basis of characters and plots of the Palliser novels has tended to fade, as readers have grown more interested in Trollope's politics as a broadly based critique of Victorian society.

This theme is not developed in isolation from other central preoccupations in Trollope's work, including his persistent concern with national characteristics and international dynamics, and with gender, courtship, and marriage. In the character of Phineas Finn, Irishness interacts with a partly feminized nature to define Phineas's tense relations with a political world which eventually accepts his value. Critic Matthew Sussman, discussing Frederik Van Dam's influential account of Trollope's late style, speaks of his writing as 'a way of inhabiting the linguistic and cultural conventions of Victorian liberalism while simultaneously subverting, satirizing, and estranging them'. Sussman's comment encapsulates the positive response to the layered complexities of Trollope's cultural and national politics that has characterized the ways in which his standing has changed in the 21st century.

Fresh appreciations of Trollope's achievements in narrative technique, and as a stylist, have also contributed to his growing reputation. Critics and readers who were once inclined to take at face value his self-deprecating accounts of his style as nothing more than a simple and transparent vehicle for narrative are now more likely to appreciate the subtleties of the fluid relations between author and audience that develop in his fiction, and of the ways in which he insists that his readers exercise their own faculties of judgement in responding to the dilemmas and difficulties faced by his characters. A clearer recognition of the uncertainties of Trollope's politics, which were not defined by the boundaries of either liberalism or conservatism, has informed a changing response to his stimulatingly open and often challenging style.

Anthony Trollope

This association has influenced recent scholarly approaches to his work, as they examine the equivocations that lay at the heart of Victorian liberalism, but it has been equally important to readers outside academia, who find in Trollope's fiction a thought-provoking point of entry into the recalcitrant moral conundrums that continue to haunt contemporary life. How should young women and men find their place in the world? What part should the desire for money or social status play in their ambitions? How might political realism coexist with idealism? Trollope's belief in the values of honesty and compassion continues to offer a firm framework for his readers' engagement, but neither his characters nor his readers find easy solutions as they pursue answers to these challenging problems. Trollope is not always a comfortable writer, but the rich pleasures and rewards of his complex imaginative world are undiminished for succeeding generations of readers. He is here to stay.

Timeline

Note: Selected publications are noted here, with the date of completed volume publication given.

1815	Born at 16 Keppel Street, London, on 24 April
1823	Enters Harrow School
1825	Attends Arthur Drury's school at Sunbury
1827	Enters Winchester College
1830	After returning home, re-enters Harrow School
1834	Leaves school; accompanies family in escaping creditors at Bruges; takes up post as junior clerk in the Post Office
1841	Secures post as deputy postal surveyor's clerk at Bannagher, Ireland
1843	Begins first novel, *The Macdermots of Ballycloran*
1844	Marries Rose Heseltine (d. 1917); moves to Southern District of Ireland as assistant surveyor
1846	First son (Henry Merivale Trollope, d. 1926) born
1847	*The Macdermots of Ballycloran*. Second son (Frederick James Anthony Trollope, d. 1910) born
1848	*The Kellys and the O'Kellys*
1850	*La Vendée*
1851	Travels on behalf of the Post Office in England and Wales
1852	Recommends the adoption of pillar-boxes for post on the Channel Islands

1854	Becomes Post Office surveyor for Northern District of Ireland
1855	*The Warden*
1857	*Barchester Towers*
1858	*Doctor Thorne. The Three Clerks.* Visits Egypt, the Holy Land, Malta, Gibraltar, Spain, the West Indies, and Central America
1859	*The West Indies and the Spanish Main.* Visits North America (New York), and Canada. Transferred to the Eastern District of England; moves to Waltham House, Waltham Cross, Hertfordshire
1860	Meets Kate Field
1861	*Framley Parsonage. Tales of All Countries*
1862	*Orley Farm. North America.* Elected to the Garrick Club
1863	*Tales of All Countries Second Series.* Visits Switzerland and Germany
1864	*The Small House at Allington.* Elected to the Athenaeum Club
1865	*Can You Forgive Her? Miss Mackenzie*
1866	*Clergymen of the Church of England*
1867	*The Last Chronicle of Barset.* Resigns from the Post Office. Begins to edit *Saint Pauls: A Monthly Magazine*
1868	Visits North America. Loses election as the Liberal candidate for Beverley, Yorkshire
1869	*He Knew He Was Right. Phineas Finn*
1870	*The Vicar of Bullhampton. The Commentaries of Caesar.* Resigns as editor of *Saint Pauls*
1871	*Ralph the Heir.* Visits Australia, New Zealand, Honolulu, and North America. Moves to Montague Square
1872	*The Eustace Diamonds*
1873	*Australia and New Zealand*
1874	*Phineas Redux*
1875	*The Way We Live Now.* Visits Italy, Ceylon, Australia, and North America. Begins *An Autobiography* on the voyage home

1876	*The Prime Minister.* Completes *An Autobiography;* leaves instructions for publication after his death
1877	*The American Senator.* Visits South Africa
1878	*Is He Popenjoy? South Africa*
1879	*Thackeray. Cousin Henry. John Caldigate*
1880	*The Duke's Children. The Life of Cicero.* Moves to South Harting, Sussex
1881	*Dr Wortle's School*
1882	*The Fixed Period. Lord Palmerston.* Visits Ireland. Suffers stroke, and dies on 6 December
1883	*An Autobiography*

References and further reading

General further reading

The story of Anthony Trollope's enterprising and restless life is almost as absorbing as his fiction. Readers looking to learn more should begin with his autobiography. It provides fascinating insights, and though it damaged his reputation in the years immediately following his death, it has since become central to assessments of his achievement. T. H. S. Escott's work has the advantage of drawing on personal interviews with Trollope. As interest in his work gathered momentum in the late 1980s and 1990s, a cluster of excellent biographies, each with distinctive strengths, began to transform perceptions of his achievement. R. H. Super drew attention to inaccuracies in previous studies, while Richard Mullen placed Trollope in a wider social and cultural context. N. John Hall's sympathetic biography draws on his comprehensive edition of Trollope's letters, and Victoria Glendinning's lively account made his writing more immediately accessible to a new generation of readers. The Trollope Society <https://trollopesociety.org/> provides much detailed information about Trollope's life and work, alongside frequent events (online and in person) to discuss his continuing legacy.

Critics began to take Trollope more seriously in the later decades of the 20th century, developing fresh and productive approaches to his work in the context of growing interest in issues of gender, imperialism, travel writing, professionalization, or literary style. A series of 'Companions' offer helpful introductions to these challenging and constructive developments. Numerous general studies have appeared—including James Kincaid's important overview, Walter Kendrick's study of Trollope's social realism, and Stephen Wall's absorbing account of Trollope's characterization. Introductions to the Oxford World's Classics editions of Trollope's novels supply invaluable information and interpretative guidance to readers. Selected studies that explore more specific areas of interest are listed under the chapter headings below.

Biography

T. H. S. Escott, *Anthony Trollope: His Work, Associates and Literary Originals* (London: The Bodley Head, 1913).

Victoria Glendinning, *Anthony Trollope* (New York: Alfred A. Knopf, 1992).

N. John Hall, *Trollope: A Biography* (Oxford: Clarendon Press, 1991).

Richard Mullen, *Anthony Trollope: A Victorian in his World* (London: Duckworth, 1990).

R. H. Super, *The Chronicler of Barsetshire: A Life of Anthony Trollope* (Ann Arbor: University of Michigan Press, 1988).

Anthony Trollope, *The Letters of Anthony Trollope*, ed. N. John Hall, with the assistance of Nina Burgis, 2 vols (Stanford, Calif.: Stanford University Press, 1983).

Anthony Trollope, *An Autobiography and Other Writings*, ed. Nicholas Shrimpton (Oxford: Oxford University Press, 2014).

Criticism

Carolyn Dever and Lisa Niles (eds), *The Cambridge Companion to Anthony Trollope* (Cambridge: Cambridge University Press, 2011).

Walter M. Kendrick, *The Novel-Machine: The Theory and Fiction of Anthony Trollope* (Baltimore and London: Johns Hopkins University Press, 1980).

James Kincaid, *The Novels of Anthony Trollope* (Oxford: Clarendon Press, 1977).

Deborah Denenholz Morse, Margaret Markwick, and Mark Turner (eds), *The Routledge Research Companion to Anthony Trollope* (London and New York: Routledge, 2017).

Richard Mullen and James Munson (eds), *The Penguin Companion to Trollope* (London: Penguin, 1996).

R. C. Terry (ed.), *The Oxford Reader's Companion to Trollope* (Oxford: Oxford University Press, 1999).

Frederik Van Dam, David Skilton, and Ortwin de Graef (eds), *The Edinburgh Companion to Anthony Trollope* (Edinburgh: Edinburgh University Press, 2019).

Stephen Wall, *Trollope and Character* (London: Faber and Faber, 1988).

Preface

Alan Johnson, *Guardian*, 11 April 2015.

Harold Macmillan, quoted in Peter Catterall, 'The Prime Minister and His Trollope: Reading Harold Macmillan's Reading', *Cercles Occasional Papers* 1 (2004), 6, 16–17.

Chapter 1: Family and work

Helen Heineman, *Mrs Trollope: The Triumphant Feminine in the Nineteenth Century* (Athens: Ohio University Press, 1979).

Thomas Babington Macaulay, 'Von Ranke', *Edinburgh Review* 72 (1840), 227–58.

Richard Salmon, *The Formation of the Victorian Literary Profession* (Cambridge: Cambridge University Press, 2013).

Nicholas Shrimpton, 'Introduction', in Anthony Trollope, *An Autobiography and Other Writings* (Oxford: Oxford University Press, 2014).

David Skilton, 'Reading *An Autobiography* as Advice Literature', in Frederik Van Dam, David Skilton, and Ortwin de Graef (eds), *The Edinburgh Companion to Anthony Trollope* (Edinburgh: Edinburgh University Press, 2019), 79–90.

Thomas Adolphus Trollope, *What I Remember*, 3 vols (London: Richard Bentley and Son, 1887–9).

Chapter 2: Story and style

Amanda Anderson, 'Trollope's Modernity', *ELH* 74 (2007), 509–34.

Dinah Birch, 'Fiction and the Law: Stylistic Uncertainties in Trollope's *Orley Farm*', in Daniel Tyler (ed.), *On Style in Victorian Fiction* (Cambridge: Cambridge University Press, 2022), 191–208.

Lewis Carroll, *Alice's Adventures in Wonderland*, ed. Peter Hunt (Oxford: Oxford University Press, 2009).

N. John Hall, *Trollope and His Illustrators* (London: Macmillan, 1980).

Christopher Herbert, *Trollope and Comic Pleasure* (Chicago: University of Chicago Press, 1987).

Robert Tracy, *Trollope's Later Novels* (Berkeley: University of California Press), 1978.

Anthony Trollope, *Thackeray* (London: Macmillan & Co., 1879).

Anthony Trollope, *The New Zealander*, ed. N. John Hall (Oxford: The Clarendon Press, 1972).

Frederik Van Dam, *Anthony Trollope's Late Style: Victorian Liberalism and Literary Form* (Edinburgh: Edinburgh University Press, 2016).

Chapter 3: Ireland

Melissa Fegan, *Literature and the Irish Famine* (Oxford: Oxford University Press, 2002).

Roy Foster, *The Irish Times*, 25 July 2015.

R. H. Hutton, *Spectator* 52 (1879), 210.

Helen Garlinghouse King (ed.), 'Trollope's Letters to the Examiner', *Princeton University Library Chronicle* 26 (1965), 75–101; 83, 75.

John McCourt, *Writing the Frontier: Anthony Trollope between Britain and Ireland* (Oxford: Oxford University Press, 2015).

Michael Sadleir, *Trollope: A Commentary*, 3rd edn (Oxford: Oxford University Press, 1961), 148.

Victorian Literature and Culture 32 (2004). A special issue on Trollope and Ireland, with important articles by Laura M. Berol, Jane Elizabeth Dougherty, Patrick Lonergan, and Bridget Matthews-Kane.

Chapter 4: Chronicling Barsetshire

Elizabeth A. Bridgham, *Spaces of the Sacred and the Profane: Dickens, Trollope and the Victorian Cathedral Town* (New York: Routledge, 2008).

Jill Felicity Durey, *Trollope and the Church of England* (New York: Palgrave Macmillan, 2002).

Elizabeth Gaskell, *The Letters of Mrs Gaskell*, ed. J. A. V. Chapple and Arthur Pollard (Manchester: Manchester University Press, 1966), 602.

Margaret Oliphant, 'Novels', *Blackwood's Magazine* 102 (1867), 277–8.

Mary Poovey, 'Trollope's Barsetshire Series', in Carolyn Dever and Lisa
Niles (eds), *The Cambridge Companion to Anthony Trollope*
(Cambridge: Cambridge University Press, 2011), 31–44.

W. M. Thackeray, 'A Letter from the Editor to a Friend and
Contributor', cited in G. N. Ray (ed.), *The Letters and Private Papers
of W. M. Thackeray*, 4 vols (Oxford: Oxford University Press, 1943),
vol. 4, 160–2.

Anthony Trollope, *Clergymen of the Church of England* (London:
Chapman & Hall, 1866).

Anthony Trollope, *The Letters of Anthony Trollope*, ed. N. John Hall,
2 vols (Stanford, Calif.: Stanford University Press, 1983),
vol. 1, 45–6; 51–2.

Unsigned review, *Saturday Review* 11 (1861), 451–2.

Chapter 5: Politics and power in the Palliser novels

William A. Cohen, 'The Palliser Novels', in Carolyn Dever and Lisa
Niles (eds), *The Cambridge Companion to Anthony Trollope*
(Cambridge: Cambridge University Press, 2011), 44–57.

Nicholas Dames, 'Trollope and the Career: Vocational Trajectories
and the Management of Ambition', *Victorian Studies*
45 (2003), 247–78.

Charles Dickens, *Great Expectations*, ed. Margaret Cardwell and
Robert Douglas-Fairhurst (Oxford: Oxford University Press, 2008).

John Halperin, *Trollope and Politics: A Study of the Pallisers and
Others* (London: Macmillan, 1977).

Linda C. McClain, 'A "Woman's Best Right"—To a Husband or the
Ballot? Political and Household Governance in Anthony Trollope's
Palliser Novels', *Boston University Law Review* 100 (2020), 1861–95.

Juliet McMaster, *Trollope's Palliser Novels: Theme and Pattern*
(London: Macmillan, 1978).

John Henry Newman, *The Idea of a University*, ed. Ian Ker (Oxford:
Oxford University Press, 1976), 179.

Anthony Trollope, *Lord Palmerston* (London: Isbister, 1882).

Chapter 6: Money, inheritance, and the law

Marc Arkin, 'Trollope and the Law', *The New Criterion* 26 (2007),
23–30.

Paul Delany, *Literature, Money and the Market: From Trollope to Amis*
(London: Palgrave, 2002).

Coral Lansbury, *The Reasonable Man: Trollope's Legal Fiction* (Princeton: Princeton University Press, 1981).

R. D. McMaster, *Trollope and the Law* (New York: St Martin's, 1986).

Francis O'Gorman (ed.), *Victorian Literature and Finance* (Oxford: Oxford University Press, 2007).

Meredith White Townsend, *The Spectator* 48 (1875), 825.

Anthony Trollope, *The Letters of Anthony Trollope*, ed. N. John Hall, 2 vols (Stanford, Calif.: Stanford University Press, 1983), vol. 2, 548.

Chapter 7: Women and men

Kate Flint, 'Queer Trollope', in Carolyn Dever and Lisa Niles (eds), *The Cambridge Companion to Anthony Trollope* (Cambridge: Cambridge University Press, 2011), 99–113.

Margaret Markwick, *New Men in Trollope's Novels: Rewriting the Victorian Male* (Aldershot: Ashgate, 2007).

Margaret Markwick, Deborah Denenholz Morse, and Regenia Gagnier (eds), *The Politics of Gender in Anthony Trollope's Novels* (Farnham: Ashgate, 2009).

Deborah Denenholz Morse, *Women in Trollope's Palliser Novels* (Ann Arbor: UMI research, 1987).

Jane Nardin, *He Knew She Was Right: The Independent Woman in the Novels of Anthony Trollope* (Carbondale, Ill.: Southern Illinois Press, 1989).

Anthony Trollope, *The Letters of Anthony Trollope*, ed. N. John Hall, 2 vols (Stanford, Calif.: Stanford University Press, 1983), vol. 1, 175.

Chapter 8: Travel

Robert D. Aguirre, '"Affairs of State": Mobilities, Communication, and Race in Trollope's *The West Indies and the Spanish Main*', *Nineteenth-Century Contexts* 37 (2015), 1–20.

Helen Lucy Blythe, *The Victorian Colonial Romance with the Antipodes* (New York: Palgrave Macmillan, 2014), 160.

James Buzard, 'Trollope and Travel', in Carolyn Dever and Lisa Niles (eds), *The Cambridge Companion to Anthony Trollope* (Cambridge: Cambridge University Press, 2011), 168–81.

Lauren Goodlad, *The Victorian Geopolitical Aesthetic: Realism, Sovereignty, and Transnational Experience* (Oxford: Oxford University Press, 2015).

Henry James, *Partial Portraits* (London: Macmillan, 1888), 99.

Deborah Denenholz Morse, *Reforming Trollope: Race, Gender, and Englishness in the Novels of Anthony Trollope* (New York: Routledge, 2013).

Anthony Trollope, 'The Present Condition of the Northern States of the American Union', in Morris L. Parrish (ed.), *Anthony Trollope: Four Lectures* (Folcroft, Pa: Folcroft Press, 1969), 40.

Anthony Trollope, *The Collected Shorter Fiction*, ed. Julian Thompson (London: Robinson Publishing, 1992).

Anthony Trollope, *West Indies and the Spanish Main* (London: Chapman & Hall, 1859).

Anthony Trollope, *North America*, 2 vols (London: Chapman & Hall, 1862).

Anthony Trollope, *Australia and New Zealand*, 2 vols (London: Chapman & Hall, 1873).

Anthony Trollope, *The Tireless Traveller: Twenty Letters to the Liverpool Mercury* (1875; repr. Berkeley: University of California Press, 1941).

Anthony Trollope, *How the 'Mastiffs' Went to Iceland* (London: Virtue, 1878).

Anthony Trollope, *South Africa*, 2nd edn, 2 vols (London: Chapman & Hall, 1879).

Anthony Trollope, *The Letters of Anthony Trollope*, ed. N. John Hall, 2 vols (Stanford, Calif.: Stanford University Press, 1983), vol. 1, 191.

Chapter 9: Afterlife

BBC online, The 100 Greatest British Novels, <https://www.bbc.com/culture/article/20151204-the-100-greatest-british-novels>, 2015. *The Way We Live Now* appears in 68th place; Barchester Towers is 83rd.

George Eliot, letter to Anthony Trollope, 23 October 1863, in Gordon Haight (ed.), *The George Eliot Letters*, 9 vols (New Haven: Yale University Press, 1954–78), vol. 4, 110.

Kate Flint, 'Queer Trollope', in Carolyn Dever and Lisa Niles (eds), *The Cambridge Companion to Anthony Trollope* (Cambridge: Cambridge University Press, 2011), 99–113.

Lauren M. E. Goodlad, *The Victorian Geopolitical Aesthetic: Realism, Sovereignty, and Transnational Experience* (Oxford: Oxford University Press, 2015), 65–86.

Linda C. McClain and Allison Tait, 'Household Intimacy and
    Being Unmarried: Family Pluralism in the Novels of Anthony
    Trollope', *Washington Journal of Law & Policy* 72 (2023), 51–102.
Robert McCrum, *Guardian*, 17 February 2014.
Margaret Markwick, Deborah Denenholz Morse, and Regenia Gagnier
    (eds), *The Politics of Gender in Anthony Trollope's Novels: New
    Readings for the Twenty-First Century* (Aldershot and Burlington:
    Ashgate, 2009), 8.
Matthew Sussman, Review of Frederik Van Dam, 'Anthony Trollope's
    Late Style: Victorian Liberalism and Literary Form' (Edinburgh
    University Press, 2016), *The Review of English Studies* 67 (2016),
    1016–18.
Anthony Trollope, *The Letters of Anthony Trollope*, ed.
    N. John Hall, 2 vols (Stanford, Calif.: Stanford University Press,
    1983), vol. 2, 886.
Virginia Woolf, 'Phases of Fiction', *Collected Essays*, 4 vols (London:
    Chatto and Windus, 1966), vol. 2, 57.

Index

For the benefit of digital users, indexed terms that span two pages (e.g., 52–53) may, on occasion, appear on only one of those pages.

ARISTOTLE
A Very Short Introduction
Jonathan Barnes

The influence of Aristotle, the prince of philosophers, on the intellectual history of the West is second to none. In this *Very Short Introduction* Jonathan Barnes examines Aristotle's scientific research, his discoveries in logic, his metaphysical theories, his work in psychology, ethics, and politics, and his ideas about art and poetry, placing his teachings in their historical context.

> 'With compressed verve, Jonathan Barnes displays the extraordinary versatility of Aristotle, the great systematising empiricist.'

> Sunday Times

BESTSELLERS
A Very Short Introduction
John Sutherland

'I rejoice', said Doctor Johnson, 'to concur with the Common Reader.' For the last century, the tastes and preferences of the common reader have been reflected in the American and British bestseller lists, and this *Very Short Introduction* takes an engaging look through the lists to reveal what we have been reading - and why. John Sutherland shows that bestseller lists monitor one of the strongest pulses in modern literature and are therefore worthy of serious study. Along the way, he lifts the lid on the bestseller industry, examines what makes a book into a bestseller, and asks what separates bestsellers from canonical fiction.

'His amiable trawl through the history of popular books is frequently entertaining'

Scott Pack, The Times

www.oup.com/vsi

BIOGRAPHY
A Very Short Introduction
Hermione Lee

Biography is one of the most popular, best-selling, and widely-read of literary genres. But why do certain people and historical events arouse so much interest? How can biographies be compared with history and works of fiction? Does a biography need to be true? Is it acceptable to omit or conceal things? Does the biographer need to personally know the subject? Must a biographer be subjective? In this *Very Short Introduction* Hermione Lee considers the cultural and historical background of different types of biographies, looking at the factors that affect biographers and whether there are different strategies, ethics, and principles required for writing about one person compared to another. She also considers contemporary biographical publications and considers what kind of 'lives' are the most popular and in demand.

> 'It would be hard to think of anyone better to provide a crisp contribution to OUP's Very Short Introductions.'

> **Kathryn Hughes, The Guardian**

ROMANTICISM
A Very Short Introduction
Michael Ferber

What is Romanticism? In this *Very Short Introduction*
Michael Ferber answers this by considering who the romantics
were and looks at what they had in common – their ideas, beliefs,
commitments, and tastes. He looks at the birth and growth
of Romanticism throughout Europe and the Americas, and
examines various types of Romantic literature, music, painting,
religion, and philosophy. Focusing on topics, Ferber looks at the
rising prestige of the poet; Romanticism as a religious trend;
Romantic philosophy and science; Romantic responses to the
French Revolution; and the condition of women. Using examples
and quotations he presents a clear insight into this very diverse
movement.

www.oup.com/vsi

GERMAN LITERATURE
A Very Short Introduction
Nicholas Boyle

German writers, from Luther and Goethe to Heine, Brecht, and Günter Grass, have had a profound influence on the modern world. This *Very Short Introduction* presents an engrossing tour of the course of German literature from the late Middle Ages to the present, focussing especially on the last 250 years. Emphasizing the economic and religious context of many masterpieces of German literature, it highlights how they can be interpreted as responses to social and political changes within an often violent and tragic history. The result is a new and clear perspective which illuminates the power of German literature and the German intellectual tradition, and its impact on the wider cultural world.

> 'Boyle has a sure touch and an obvious authority... this is a balanced and lively introduction to German literature.'
>
> Ben Hutchinson, TLS

RUSSIAN LITERATURE
A Very Short Introduction
Catriona Kelly

Rather than a conventional chronology of Russian literature, Catriona Kelly's *Very Short Introduction* explores the place and importance of diverse literature in Russian culture. How and when did a Russian national literature come into being? What shaped its creation? How have the Russians regarded their literary language? At the centre of the web is the figure of Pushkin, 'the Russian Shakespeare', whose work influenced all Russian writers, whether poets or novelists, and many great artists in other areas as well.

'brilliant and original, taking an unexpected approach to the subject, and written with great confidence and clarity.'

Peter France, University of Edinburgh

'a great pleasure to read. It is a sophisticated, erudite, searching, and subtle piece of work. It is written in a lively and stimulating manner, and displays a range to which few of Dr Kelly's peers in the field of Russian scholarship can aspire.'

Phil Cavendish, School of Slavonic and East European Studies, University of London

www.oup.com/vsi

FRENCH LITERATURE
A Very Short Introduction
John D. Lyons

The heritage of literature in the French language is rich,
varied, and extensive in time and space; appealing both to its
immediate public, readers of French, and also to aglobal
audience reached through translations and film adaptations.
French Literature: A Very Short Introduction introduces this lively
literary world by focusing on texts - epics, novels, plays, poems,
and screenplays - that concern protagonists whose adventures
and conflicts reveal shifts in literary and social practices. From
the hero of the medieval *Song of Roland* to the Caribbean
heroines of *Tituba, Black Witch of Salem* or the European
expatriate in Japan in *Fear and Trembling*, these problematic
protagonists allow us to understand what interests writers and
readers across the wide world of French.

www.oup.com/vsi

UTOPIANISM
A Very Short Introduction
Lyman Tower Sargent

This *Very Short Introduction* explores utopianism and its history. Lyman Sargent discusses the role of utopianism in literature, and in the development of colonies and in immigration. The idea of utopia has become commonplace in social and political thought, both negatively and positively. Some thinkers see a trajectory from utopia to totalitarianism with violence an inevitable part of the mix. Others see utopia directly connected to freedom and as a necessary element in the fight against totalitarianism. In Christianity utopia is labelled as both heretical and as a fundamental part of Christian belief, and such debates are also central to such fields as architecture, town and city planning, and sociology among many others.

www.oup.com/vsi

WILLIAM SHAKESPEARE
A Very Short Introduction
Stanley ells

In this new offering from Stanley Wells, the pre-eminent
Shakespearian scholar, comes an exploration of one of the
world's greatest dramatists: William Shakespeare.

Examining Shakespeare's narrative poems, sonnets, and all of his
plays, Wells outlines their sources, style, and originality over the
course of Shakespeare's career, to consider the fundamental
impact his work has had for subsequent generations. Written
with enthusiasm and flair by a scholar who has devoted a lifetime
to the study of Shakespeare and his works, this is an engaging
and authoritative introduction that looks at both the world
Shakespeare lived in and all of his major works, to show how
and why he continues to be so influential and important to
society today.

"this is an excellent place to start exploring the life and work of
probably the most celebrated dramatist not only in Britain but
also throughout the world." - Shiny New Books

www.oup.com/vsi

WRITING AND SCRIPT
A Very Short Introduction
Andrew Robinson

Without writing, there would be no records, no history, no books, and no emails. Writing is an integral and essential part of our lives; but when did it start? Why do we all write differently and how did writing develop into what we use today? All of these questions are answered in this *Very Short Introduction*. Starting with the origins of writing five thousand years ago, with cuneiform and Egyptian hieroglyphs, Andrew Robinson explains how these early forms of writing developed into hundreds of scripts including the Roman alphabet and the Chinese characters.

'User-friendly survey.'

Steven Poole, The Guardian

www.oup.com/vsi